Conc:
Gai
Bird
Guide

There are 47 individual Wildlife Trusts covering the whole of the UK and the Isle of Man and Alderney. Together The Wildlife Trusts are the largest UK voluntary organization dedicated to protecting wildlife and wild places everywhere – at land and sea. They are supported by 791,000 members, 150,000 of whom belong to their junior branch, Wildlife Watch. Every year The Wildlife Trusts work with thousands of schools, and their nature reserves and visitor centres receive millions of visitors.

The Wildlife Trusts work in partnership with hundreds of landowners and businesses in the UK. Building on their existing network of 2,250 nature reserves, The Wildlife Trusts' recovery plan for the UK's wildlife and fragmented habitats, known as A Living Landscape, is being achieved through restoring, recreating and reconnecting large areas of wildlife habitat.

The Wildlife Trusts also have a vision for the UK's seas and sea life – Living Seas, in which wildlife thrives from the depths of the oceans to the coastal shallows. In Living Seas, wildlife and habitats are recovering, the natural environment is adapting well to a changing climate, and people are inspired by marine wildlife and value the sea for the many ways in which it supports our quality of life. As well as protecting wildlife, these projects help to safeguard the ecosystems we depend on for services like clean air and water.

All 47 Wildlife Trusts are members of the Royal Society of Wildlife Trusts (Registered charity number 207238). To find your local Wildlife Trust visit wildlifetrusts.org

Concise
Garden
Bird
Guide

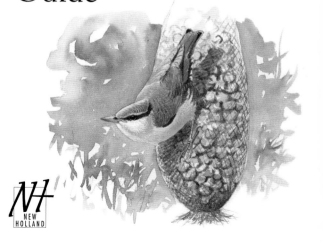

NH
NEW
HOLLAND

First published in 2012 by New Holland Publishers (UK) Ltd
London · Cape Town · Sydney · Auckland
www.newhollandpublishers.com

Garfield House, 86–88 Edgware Road, London W2 2EA, UK
80 McKenzie Street, Cape Town 8001, South Africa
Unit 1, 66 Gibbes Street, Chatswood, New South Wales 2067, Australia
218 Lake Road, Northcote, Auckland, New Zealand

10 9 8 7 6 5 4 3 2 1

ISBN 978 1 84773 978 0

Series Editor: Krystyna Mayer
Design: Alan Marshall
Artworks: Dan Cole, Sandra Doyle, David Daly, Bridgette James,
 Szabolcs Kokay, Stephen Message & David Sutton
Production: Melanie Dowland
Publisher: Simon Papps

The publishers thank Amy Lewis of The Wildlife Trusts for reading the text.

Reproduction by Modern Age Repro Co. Ltd., Hong Kong
Printed and bound in China by Leo Paper Group

Other titles in series

Contents

Introduction

The *Concise Garden Bird Guide* is first and foremost a garden bird identification guide containing detailed descriptions of the most commonly encountered species, as well as some rarities and birds you may only see flying overhead in gardens. It also includes general guidelines on food, feeders, nest boxes and other items that can greatly increase the presence of birds in gardens. More detailed information on the practical elements of creating a bird-friendly garden, such as making nest boxes and gardening for wildlife, is available in books devoted specifically to these purposes.

Attracting Birds

You can entice birds to even the smallest garden by putting out foods such as seeds, grains and kitchen scraps. They are also attracted to berry-bearing shrubs and trees, particularly in autumn and winter, and by the insects that feed on plants. Native plants are generally better food sources than introduced ones, although non-native plants such as cotoneasters and pyracanthas, which produce large amounts of fruits in autumn, are just as useful as native species. In larger gardens, plants that are particularly good for attracting birds but are considered invasive, such as Teasels and Common Nettles, can be grown in specially dedicated wilderness areas.

Even the smallest pond attracts insects and other invertebrates, and provides birds with an additional source of food. A pond may provide a place for birds to drink and bathe if it has shallow areas at the edges; a smaller water source such as a bird bath serves this function very well.

Dense shrubs and trees provide cover for shelter and nesting, as well as food. Shelter in the form of nest boxes attracts birds, but they will only nest if there is enough small insect food available nearby, because even the seed-eating species feed their young on insects.

Birds that are nesting should not be disturbed. Bear in mind that it is illegal to approach or inspect artificial or natural nests where birds are nesting (generally early March–late August). It is also illegal to carry out tree surgery where nesting birds are present.

Identifying Birds

The information in this book includes the size of each featured species in average length, variations in plumage colours, calls and songs, habitat details and aspects of behaviour. Many birds can be tricky to identify even for the most experienced birdwatcher. When attempting to identify a bird, check the following distinguishing characteristics:

Flight This can be a major identification clue. As examples, woodland birds such as woodpeckers have an undulating flight that is particularly noticeable when they are flying across an open area; Kingfishers have a fast and direct flight, often close to the surface of water; ducks and swans fly with rapidly moving pointed wings and outstretched necks.

Shape General shape and distinguishing characteristics such as the bill shape (page 9), and tail or leg length.

Colour and plumage patterns Some birds, such as Mute Swans, are distinctive and relatively easy to identify. However, colour and plumage patterns are not always the best guides to identification. Male birds often differ from female birds, juveniles generally differ from their parents (and often from each other), and the plumage of many birds varies depending on the time of the year and the light conditions. Some species, such as Willow Warblers and Common Chiffchaffs (page 8), are very similar and may be particularly difficult to identify.

Willow Warbler (above) and Common Chiffchaff (below), are difficult to tell apart – voice is often the best method

Behaviour Many birds, such as tits, are gregarious and often likely to be seen in flocks, particularly during winter, while others are more frequently seen in pairs. It is also useful to look at the way a bird is feeding and relating to other birds.

Noise Although some bird calls and songs are quite obvious and easy to learn, others are more difficult. The 'quack' of a Mallard, the soft cooing of a feral pigeon and the strident calls of gulls are familiar sounds to many people, but warblers, with their various similar-sounding calls, can take many years to achieve familiarity with.

Bill Shapes

Birds have evolved a variety of bill shapes according to the food that they eat. In general, birds with thin bills are insect eaters, those with thick bills seed eaters. Birds in these categories do, however, vary their diets. Nestlings of seed-eating birds such as House Sparrows are fed on grubs and soft insects, and thin-billed tits happily eat peanuts. Other bill variations include the broad and sharp-edged bills of Bullfinches for stripping buds and crushing fruits and seeds; the 'all-purpose' bills of thrushes for eating a wide variety of foods; and the sturdy hooked bills of birds of prey such as Sparrowhawks, which are suited to tearing up flesh.

BILLS OF TYPICAL INSECT EATERS

Sedge Warbler

Common
Chiffchaff

Spotted Flycatcher
(juvenile)

BILLS OF TYPICAL SEED EATERS

Lesser Redpoll

Goldfinch

OTHER BILL TYPES

Sparrowhawk

Bullfinch

Blackbird

Plants for Birds

TREES, SHRUBS & FLOWERING PLANTS

Plants provide food for birds in the form of insects, seeds and autumn fruits. Large plants such as trees and shrubs also offer cover, shelter and nesting places. Examples of plants that attract birds are shown on the following pages.

Elder *Sambucus niger* Deciduous tree to 10m tall. Large clusters of heavily scented creamy-white flowers, followed by purple-red berries in August– September. Flowers are popular with nectar-feeding insects, fed on by birds in summer, and the berries attract birds such as thrushes. Gives good cover for nesting birds.

Goat Willow *Salix caprea* Usually to about 12m tall. Catkins about 3cm long. Fruits ripen in May–June and are followed by woolly seeds. Attracts numerous insects. Leaves are eaten by larvae and support many aphids and sawflies, all of which are important to birds.

Common Alder *Alnus glutinosa* To about 25m tall. Favourite food source for many birds, such as Siskins and Lesser Redpolls, which feed on the catkins in spring and the seed cones in autumn–winter.

Common Hawthorn *Craetegus monogyna*

Dense, thorny deciduous tree to 16m tall, often grown in hedgerows. Offers protection for nesting birds. Small, dark red autumn berries (haws) provide food for finches and thrushes. Clusters of creamy-white flowers attract numerous insects in spring–summer, which are eaten by birds. Larvae of many moth species feed on the leaves and are themselves a food source for birds.

Pendunculate Oak *Quercus robur* Massive deciduous tree to 45m tall. Male flowers form long catkins in spring, and acorns appear in stalked clusters in autumn. Mature oaks are habitats for thousands of creatures,

including insects and other invertebrates, which are a valuable food source for birds particularly when they are nesting in spring. They offer suitable sites for nesting, including cavities for hole-nesting birds such as tits. Acorns are favoured by birds like Jays and Nuthatches.

Wild Crab *Malus sylvestris* Small tree to 9m tall. A parent species of cultivated apples. White or pink flowers in spring and small greenish fruits in autumn. In spring the

flowers attract insects that provide food for nesting birds. Windfall fruits of different varieties of apple are an invaluable food source for birds such as Redwings and Fieldfares in hard weather.

Holly *Ilex aquifolium* Evergreen shrub or small tree to 25m tall, often used as hedging. Dark green leaves with sharp spines. Flowers in spring, followed by bright red berries in autumn. Dense foliage provides cover for roosting and nesting. Berries are popular with birds such as thrushes.

Honeysuckle *Lonicera periclymenum* Deciduous climber with sweetly scented, creamy-white flowers suffused with red or purple, followed by red berries. Established honeysuckles provide good nesting sites for thrushes. They attract aphids, which are an important food source for birds, and the berries are fed on by warblers, thrushes and finches.

Common Ivy *Hedera helix* Self-clinging evergreen climber with woody stems that can grow to 20m in length. Yellowish-green flowers in globular heads, then berries that darken to purplish-black. Ivies provide food and shelter for birds all year round. Mature plants may shelter Wren nests. In summer the flowers attract many insects that are a source of food for birds, and in autumn the fruits attract berry-loving birds such as thrushes.

Dog-rose *Rosa canina* Scrambling deciduous small shrub about 3m tall, with stems covered in thorns. Large pink or whitish flowers; fruit is an ovoid bright red hip. More than 200 insect species feed on roses, and they attract aphids, which are an important part of many birds' diets. Hips attract warblers, thrushes and finches in autumn.

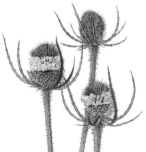

Teasel *Dipsacus fullonum* Robust prickly biennial to 2m tall. Good plant for a garden wilderness area. Flowers July–August. Produces spiky seed-heads. One species of bird in particular, the Goldfinch, has evolved a very sharp bill for extracting seeds from the heads.

Blackberry *Anthriscus sylvestris*
Perennial to 3m tall, with very prickly, arching stems, pink or white flowers and fruits ripening from red to black. Also known as Bramble. Grows in scrub, hedgerows and woods. An invasive plant most suitable for a wild area of a garden. Provides excellent cover for nesting birds such as Dunnocks. Autumn blackberry crop attracts a variety of birds, including whitethroats and thrushes.

Primrose *Primula vulgaris* Clump-forming perennial with usually pale yellow flowers (garden varieties are available in a wider range of colours). Flowers are solitary and borne on long stalks. They attract a host of insects, and in autumn the seeds are eaten by birds such as finches.

Common Nettle *Urtica dioica* Upright perennial to 1.5m tall, covered with stinging hairs. Invasive and thus best grown in clumps in a wild area of a garden. Flowers are small and greenish. Attracts numerous insects, including caterpillars, and produces many seeds in autumn, both of great value to birds.

Meadow Buttercup *Ranunculus acris* Distinctive and familiar perennial to 1m tall. Classic meadow plant producing bright yellow flowers from spring to autumn. Flowers attract all kinds of tiny insect.

Common Poppy *Papaver rhoeas* Striking annual to 70cm tall, with papery flowers that are bright red. Fruit is a distinctive flat-topped capsule, the seeds released through pores beneath the cap. Flowers open in May–June and attract a host of insects. Seed-heads are an excellent food source in autumn for birds such as finches and sparrows.

Sunflower *Helianthus annus* Sunflowers grow to 5m tall and are either annual or perennial, depending on the variety. This huge and exotic-looking annual grows quickly, producing enormous dark-centred yellow flowers that may reach 30cm across and attract many insects, including hover-flies, bees and butterflies. After flowering, the seed-heads provide seeds that attract birds.

Foxglove *Digitalis purpurea* Elegant biennial or perennial to 1.8m tall. Long tubular flowers that are pinkish-purple (occasionally white) and borne on spikes. They are very popular with pollinating insects.

Drinking and Bathing

GARDEN PONDS

Almost any water body of any size will have great value for birds, for drinking, keeping cool in summer, bathing and finding food. A pond supports a large variety of invertebrates such as insects, pond snails, freshwater mussels and many tiny creatures that birds feed on. Birds also drink and bathe in shallow ponds, and may breed on larger ponds. To enable birds to drink and bathe, a pond should have a shallow end with gently sloping sides to allow them to enter the water. Vegetation should preferably be native (though not plundered from the wild). A pond should be situated away from any large trees that might drop leaves into it in the autumn, give too much shade and even damage it with their root systems.

Garden pond

BIRDBATHS

Birds' feathers need frequent cleaning to keep them in prime condition. Birdbaths are typically made of concrete or terracotta, but birds will

House Sparrow bathing in birdbath

bathe in any improvised container, such as a shallow plate or tin.

A birdbath should not be too deep to enable small birds to use it – birds do not submerge their entire bodies, only dipping their wings to splash water on to their backs. It should ideally have a shallow and deeper end to allow small birds such as finches as well as larger birds like pigeons to use it. A rough surface will provide a grip and prevent birds from slipping. The birdbath should be on a stand of about a metre tall, and positioned in an open area with about a metre of clear space on all sides in order to minimize predators. The water should be changed every day or so to prevent algae, as well as bacteria that may cause disease, from forming in it.

Redpolls using birdbath on a stand

DUST BATHS

Some birds like to rid their plumage of parasites and keep their feathers clean by dust-bathing. While taking a dust bath, they cower close to the ground and wiggle their bodies, spreading one or both wings (shown on page 165). This is often followed by preening and shaking to ruffle the feathers. A shallow pit filled with sand and dusty soil can encourage birds to dust-bathe in a garden.

Feeding in Flocks

MIXED FLOCKS

Many birds begin to form flocks in late summer to early autumn. This gives them a greater opportunity of finding food than foraging by themselves, as well as affording them the best chance of avoiding predation. On a cold winter's night, they can also huddle together and provide each other with warmth. From autumn onwards, tits can be commonly seen in small parties, and heard as they utter high-pitched contact calls in order to stay together. Mixed flocks may include several species, such as Blue, Great, Coal and Long-tailed Tits, the rarer Marsh and Willow Tits, and Goldcrests, Treecreepers and even Lesser Spotted Woodpeckers. They work their way around gardens, visiting feeders as well as trees to pick up any food that is available.

Mixed flock including Long-tailed, Great and Coal Tits, as well as Goldcrests and a Treecreeper

Flock of Starlings

SINGLE-SPECIES FLOCKS

Some species do not form mixed flocks. In early evening during November–February, Starlings gather in huge flocks, known as 'murmurations', numbering tens of thousands of birds (up to 1.5 million on the Continent). They do this for safety – birds of prey find it hard to target one bird among so many; to keep warm; and to exchange information about good feeding areas.

Despite the still incredible size of flocks in Britain – the population is boosted by birds from the Continent in winter – Starlings have recently decreased by more than 70 per cent in the UK, where they are now on the critical risk of birds most at risk.

Feeding Birds

AVAILABLE BIRD FOODS

Birds benefit from receiving supplementary food in gardens year round, but particularly in winter, when natural food sources such as seeds, berries and insects may be in short supply, and during the nesting season, at the time when they feed their young. In late autumn–winter, high-fat foods such as peanuts, fat balls and cheese are helpful, while in spring and summer high-protein foods such as mealworms are valuable to birds with chicks. Avoid high-salt foods such as bacon rind, and those that may swell up inside a bird, such as desiccated coconut, and loose peanuts, which can choke young birds.

You can buy bird foods such as seeds and grain in bulk and store them in lidded bins or smaller containers in a cool, dry place. Multi-seed mixes, as well as single-ingredient foods, are available.

Black Sunflower Seeds An excellent high-energy food all year round. Available in mixed seed mixes or on their own. Oil content in black sunflower seeds is higher than in striped ones.

Sunflower Hearts Husked kernels of sunflower seeds enable quick access for birds to food that is high in calories. An additional bonus is that the messy husks are not left under a feeder.

Niger Seeds Small and black, with a high oil content. Favoured by species with slender bills such as Goldfinches, Siskins and redpolls. Require a birdfeeder with narrow delivery slits to avoid spillage of the tiny seeds.

Hemp Seeds Popular with tits, finches and sparrows, which crack the seeds open with their bills.

Millet Seeds White seeds that may attract sparrows, Dunnocks, finches, Reed Buntings and Collared Doves. High in starch and essential vitamins and minerals.

Wheat and Barley Both these grains contain vitamins, minerals and carbohydrates, and are fed on by birds such as sparrows, pigeons and pheasants.

Rolled Oats Rich source of protein and essential minerals. Higher fat and oil content than most other grains and thus ideal for use during winter. Relatively inexpensive, especially if bought in large bags, and a good food for many birds.

Peanuts Pulses unrelated to nuts that have a high oil and fat content, peanuts are one of the most energy-efficient foods available to a variety of birds. A known brand, free from aflatoxin – a naturally occurring chemical from a fungus produced when nuts get damp – which can kill birds, should always be bought. Peanuts are best supplied in a feeder with a wire mesh (page 28), so that a bird cannot take a whole peanut away (whole loose peanuts can choke young chicks); they are also available as granules and peanut cake. Avoid feeding birds on salted peanuts.

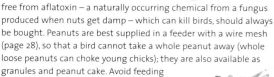

Peanut Butter Unsalted peanut butter can be put in a suspended 'peanut log'. A ready-made log with holes can be bought, or a log can be drilled with holes. Peanut butter, perhaps with nuts and seeds mixed in, can then be used to fill the holes.

Suet Products A range of fat products designed for feeding birds is available. Suet cakes in the form of balls or bars contain a combination of animal fats, seeds and sometimes insects. They can be hung from the branch of a tree and are particularly popular with smaller birds such as finches and tits. Suet 'grains' are small, high-energy pellets that can be offered straight or blended with other bird foods. Treecreepers and Nuthatches, which may go short of food during freezing weather when ice forms around trees, may take fat simply smeared onto trunks in cold weather.

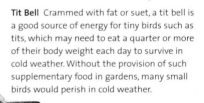

Tit Bell Crammed with fat or suet, a tit bell is a good source of energy for tiny birds such as tits, which may need to eat a quarter or more of their body weight each day to survive in cold weather. Without the provision of such supplementary food in gardens, many small birds would perish in cold weather.

Live Foods Mealworms and waxworms (the larvae of Meal Beetle and Wax Moth respectively) can attract insect-eating birds such as flycatchers, warblers, wagtails, Blackbirds and Robins to a garden. Available from specialist dealers, they can be put in a smooth-sided bowl on a bird table.

HOUSEHOLD SCRAPS

Many kitchen scraps are suitable for birds. Cut them up into tiny pieces to prevent birds from choking. Cheese, which is high in fat, is favoured by birds such as Robins, thrushes, Dunnocks and Wrens (in the latter case if grated finely). Cooked and uncooked pastry is a suitable fatty food. Brown bread, cut up into small pieces, is a good bird food, but white bread generally has little nutritional value. Cooked rice and pasta are eaten by birds, since they are full of starch; they should not be cooked with salt, which can kill birds. Cat food meat is particularly popular with Blackbirds. If you hang a bone from a tree branch, corvids such as Rooks, as well as woodpeckers, tits and Starlings, may visit to try and get at the marrow, showing surprising agility.

Clear away uneaten food regularly to prevent it from spoiling. If mice or rats are present, contain scraps in a wire-mesh basket or disused hanging basket.

Starlings feeding in wire-mesh basket containing food scraps

Rook feeding
on bone

Household scraps
including cheese
and brown bread

FRUITS

Various birds, such as thrushes and Starlings, enjoy fruits. Fresh apples, pears, bananas and grapes can be hung up or scattered on the ground. In winter clear away any snow before putting out food; hanging fruits from trees can prevent snow from obscuring the food. Fruits cut into small pieces will help birds to get to the food quickly. Dried fruits such as raisins, apricots, sultanas and currants are good foods for birds, and favourites with Blackbirds, Song Thrushes and Robins. Soak them overnight during the spring and summer months to ensure nestlings do not choke.

Thrushes such as Redwings and Fieldfares, which are winter visitors to Britain, as well as resident Blackbirds, feed on windfall apples in autumn and winter. Windfall fruits are particularly valuable energy resources for birds during hard weather.

Fresh fruits

Blackbird (top), Redwing (centre)
and Fieldfare (bottom) feeding on
windfall apples

Birdfeeders

CHOOSING BIRDFEEDERS

Many designs of birdfeeder are available. Where squirrels are a problem, use squirrel-proof feeders with a metal cage around the feeder. Cage birdfeeders designed to provide access only to smaller birds and exclude larger birds, such as feral pigeons and Woodpigeons, are also available. Like bird tables (page 30), birdfeeders should be sited near high cover. It should be possible for them to be taken apart for cleaning, which should be done regularly.

Mesh-cage Feeder Best for dispensing peanuts, these are made of steel mesh that should be about 6mm wide – large enough for birds' beaks not to be harmed and small enough to prevent whole nuts, which can choke young birds, from being taken.

Tubular Plastic Feeder Plastic tubes with holes for dispensing seeds and little perches beside each hole allowing birds to feed easily at each opening.

Fat Feeder Ready-made metal cages for pre-packed fat and seed blocks are available. Plastic mesh surrounding bought fat balls has been known to trap birds' feet and tongues; though this is a low risk, it is sensible to remove the mesh bag and dispense the fat balls from an appropriate feeder.

Window Feeder Useful in situations where there is no garden, these feeders have suckers that can be attached to window glass. They should be securely attached, so there is no danger of them falling.

Bird Tables

Basic bird table that can be fixed on a wall or tree

Open bird table on pole

Low-roofed bird table hung on tree trunk

USING A BIRD TABLE

Bird tables are useful for species that are mainly ground feeders, such as Robins, Dunnocks and Blackbirds. They should be sited away from low vegetation to reduce the risk of predation by cats. Some designs incorporate wire-mesh peanut feeders into the framework. Hanging bird tables are useful in situations where space is limited, and for discouraging unwanted visitors such as rats and squirrels, as are bird tables raised on poles. They should be placed close to high cover, which can provide concealment from predators like Sparrowhawks. Bird tables with low roofs prevent access for large birds such as pigeons, and a rim around the sides stops food from falling off. Bird tables should be scrubbed weekly to kill germs and viruses, preferably using a recommended hygiene product, then thoroughly rinsed.

Nest Boxes

GUIDELINES FOR USING NEST BOXES

Nest boxes can provide places for successful breeding in gardens that otherwise lack a range of nesting opportunities. Many different designs are available, some for specific species. Certain general rules are applicable to the positioning and care of nest boxes:

• Place sheltered from the prevailing wind and rain to avoid water from being driven into the box.

• Position away from strong sunlight to avoid overheating – which can cause the deaths of nestlings – during the hotter part of the day.

• Ensure the box is watertight from above.

• Make sure the box has easy access from the top for cleaning.

• Place in available cover to avoid the attention of predators, but ensure there is a clear flight path to the box. Wall-mounted boxes may be safer than boxes in trees, preventing access by cats and squirrels.

• Nest boxes should be at least 15mm thick for good insulation.

• Make sure the lid cannot be lifted by cats or other predators. A metal plate around the entrance hole will deter squirrels and Great Spotted Woodpeckers from attacking the hole to eat the nestlings.

• Avoid boxes with perches, which may aid access to predators.

• Fasten boxes securely to a wall, tree or post.

• Ensure a box is in a quiet spot, away from predators, children and birdfeeders. Avoid boxes with integral birdfeeders.

• The law states that it is illegal to disturb nesting birds before August. Ideally, wait until at least October before cleaning out boxes to ensure that multi-brooded birds such as sparrows have finished raising their broods. Empty the boxes and clean with boiling water (never bleach or detergent). Wear gloves to protect yourself from parasites.

• Put up a nest box in autumn or winter to give birds a chance to get used to it.

ENCLOSED BOX

Used by all kinds of hole-nesting birds, including tits, Nuthatches and flycatchers, this is the most common type of nest box. It is available in different sizes for various species. Like all nest boxes, this type is usually made of wood, although other materials may also be used. A log nest box is basically a more natural-looking enclosed box, and can be bought or self-made.

Boxes with different-size holes are suitable for different species: 25mm or larger for Blue, Coal and Marsh Tits; 28mm or larger for Great Tits, Tree Sparrows and Pied Flycatchers; 32mm for House Sparrows and Nuthatches; 45mm for Starlings. The entrance hole should be at least 120mm above the floor of the box to prevent predators from reaching inside.

Log nest box

Enclosed nest box

OPEN-FRONTED NEST BOX

Similar to the enclosed box, but
the upper half of the frontage
is left open. Frontage may be
high, medium or low. Boxes
with a medium frontage of
about 100mm high attract the
most species. Wrens may nest
in boxes with a front about
140mm high (as well as in
enclosed boxes). Open-fronted
boxes should preferably be
sited in thorny bushes or on
sheer faces such as house walls
to deny predators access.

BIRD SHELF

This version of an open-fronted nest box, with a
low front, may attract Spotted Flycatchers and
thrushes. It is most suitable for birds that
prefer an open site with good views of the
surrounding area. Bird shelves make
it easy to observe birds
raising their families.

House Martin Box

This is a bowl nest box specially designed for House Martins, though it may also be used by Swallows. The bowls can have either side or forwards-facing entrance holes. House Martins tend to nest in colonies, so putting up nests in groups may encourage more birds to build their own alongside. The boxes should be sited under the eaves of a house. Swallows nest on the ledges of buildings. Boxes intended for them are best attached to a wooden backing plate, which is fixed to a wall inside a barn or other suitable building that can be accessed by the birds at all times.

Natural House Martin nest

Artificial House Martin nest

Swallow family in artificial nest

Treecreeper nest box

Natural nest

TREECREEPER BOX

Treecreepers usually nest in a natural nook or cranny behind bark lined with a bed of tiny twigs. The nest generally has two openings, one for entry the other for exit. A wedge-shaped box with openings at the sides may encourage Treecreepers to nest in a garden.

TAWNY OWL BOX

Tawny Owls like to nest in holes in trees. A long thin box can be bought or made, then fixed to a tree, either at an angle or under a sloping branch, with nearby branches the chicks can climb over well before fledging 28–37 days after hatching. Tawny Owl boxes are only really suitable for large gardens (or woodlands). The birds are sensitive to disturbance and can be aggressive when nesting, when they are best left alone. Because of this, gardens with pets and children are generally inappropriate.

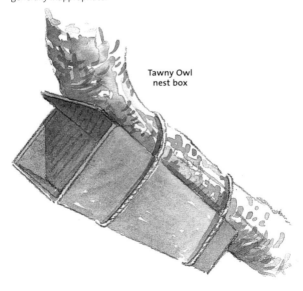

Tawny Owl nest box

**Female Kestrel
incubating eggs
in nest box**

KESTREL BOX

Kestrels tend to nest in places with open aspects on the edges of cliffs or ledges on buildings. A large open-fronted box, fixed to a pole, tree or building, preferably at least 5m from the ground, may help to replicate the natural situation. The best sites are quiet and undisturbed, within easy reach of grassland for hunting; because of this Kestrel boxes are best suited to large gardens. Tawny Owls may also nest in Kestrel boxes.

BARN OWL BOX

Barn Owls adapt readily to nest boxes and may even use them year-round as roost sites. There are different types of box available, but they all have a visible hole and a ledge underneath to prevent the fledglings from falling out. One type can be used in buildings, another on trees. If the box is fixed on a vertical surface, a rough-barked tree is more suitable than a smooth one that an owl cannot climb. Barn Owl boxes should be sited in a quiet place at least 1km away from the nearest major road (the birds may hunt on roadside verges, so are vulnerable to traffic). Barn Owls need to have clear views of suitable hunting habitats, such as open fields, so nest boxes for them are best suited to large gardens in rural areas. Never put a box in a building to which access could be cut off.

**Barn Owl
nest box**

Carrying prey
to nest

Young Barn Owls

Mute Swan
Cygnus olor

Adult   **Juvenile**

SIZE AND DESCRIPTION Length 152cm. Largest flying bird in Britain. Adult is all white, juvenile grey-brown. Orange bill with a black knob at the base (smaller in female) and a graceful curve to the neck.

VOICE Generally silent; hisses when angry or disturbed.

HABITAT AND DISTRIBUTION Almost any still or slow-moving inland water body; also estuaries and sheltered coastal regions. Found across northern and western Europe. Resident in Britain.

FOOD AND HABITS Usually feeds on water by dipping its neck below the surface, sometimes up-ending. May visit large gardens with big ponds. Nest is a large mound of plant matter on the edges of water bodies.

Mallard
Anas platyrhynchos

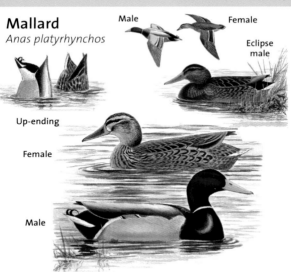

Male

Female

Eclipse male

Up-ending

Female

Male

SIZE AND DESCRIPTION Length 58cm. Britain's most common duck. Drake has a dark rich brown breast, and a dark green head with a white collar in the breeding season. Speculum (a bright, often iridescent patch of colour on the wings of some birds, especially ducks) is purple.

VOICE Ducks give the familiar 'quack'; drake has a higher-pitched call.

HABITAT AND DISTRIBUTION Resident and widespread throughout Europe, occurring on almost any inland waters other than fast-flowing rivers.

FOOD AND HABITS Surface feeding, it can be seen dabbling and up-ending. Eats a variety of food, including invertebrates, fish and plants. Birds used to humans take bread, grain and cereal. May visit large gardens with ponds or streams, or be seen flying overhead. Usually nests on the ground under bushes, close to water.

Common Pheasant
Phasianus colchicus

SIZE AND DESCRIPTION Length 75–90cm (male); 53–64cm (female). Male has a long, barred golden tail, a green head and red wattles. Some males have a white collar around the neck. Female has a shorter tail and is buffish-brown.

VOICE A loud and hoarse metallic call, 'koo-krock', then usually a whirring wingbeat.

HABITAT AND DISTRIBUTION Woodland, farmland with hedges, large gardens and reed beds in much of Europe.

FOOD AND HABITS Feeds on seeds, fruits, nuts and roots. Visits large rural gardens. Nest a grassy cup on the ground.

Female

Male

Male

Male without
white neck collar

Female searching
for food in winter

Red-legged Partridge
Alectoris rufa

SIZE AND DESCRIPTION Length 34cm. An introduced species that is a little larger than the native Grey Partridge (*Perdix perdix*). White cheeks and throat, flanks barred with white, black and chestnut, and a red bill.
VOICE Harsh 'chucka, chucka'.
HABITAT AND DISTRIBUTION Open country and farmland.
FOOD AND HABITS Mainly eats seeds and plant matter. Visits large rural gardens near its natural habitat. Nests on the ground among grass or tall vegetation, or under a bush.

Adults

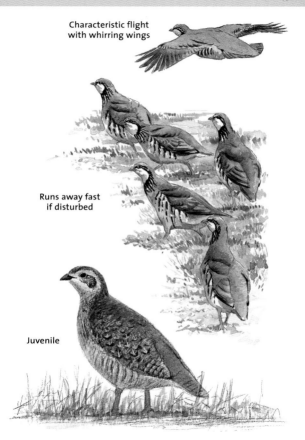

Characteristic flight
with whirring wings

Runs away fast
if disturbed

Juvenile

Grey Heron
Ardea cinerea

SIZE AND DESCRIPTION Length 95cm. Very large and mainly grey, with black-and-white markings. Breeding plumage includes long black plumes on the head. Neck is tucked back in flight; wingbeats are slow and ponderous.

VOICE Flight call a hoarse, croaking 'kraark' and 'chraa'; bill-clapping at the nest.

Juvenile

Adult

HABITAT AND DISTRIBUTION Year round in marshes, ponds, lakes, rivers, canals, flooded fields and estuaries throughout Europe.

FOOD AND HABITS Feeds on fish, amphibians, small mammals, insects and reptiles. Hunts by stalking slowly through shallow water, or standing motionless waiting for prey to come within reach, when it strikes with lightning speed. May visit gardens with ponds to hunt for fish and amphibians. Nests in colonies, usually high in tall trees, in a huge nest.

Adult

Nesting

Walking in water

Typical pose when asleep

Sparrowhawk
Accipiter nisus

SIZE AND DESCRIPTION Length 35cm. Wings blunt and broad. Male much smaller than female, and has a blue-grey head and back, and a breast barred with rusty-red. Female has grey-brown barring on the breast and a pale 'eyebrow'.

VOICE Monotonous ringing call near the nest.

HABITAT AND DISTRIBUTION Woodland, parks, gardens and hedgerows. Breeds throughout Europe. British populations are mainly resident.

FOOD AND HABITS Small birds are the main food of Sparrowhawks, which hunt by ambushing their prey. Typically a bird of open country, woodland and hedgerows, it has learned that birdfeeders put out by humans can provide an easy meal, and may hunt birds in gardens. Nest is a platform of twigs high up in the tree canopy.

Male

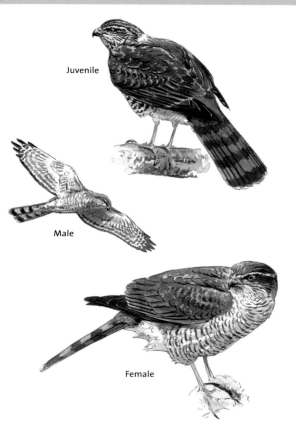

Juvenile

Male

Female

Common Buzzard
Buteo buteo

SIZE AND DESCRIPTION Length 52cm. Large with broad, rounded wings and a short tail. Usually dark brown above with variable amounts of white below; sometimes with a dark carpal patch. Soars on V-shaped wings.
VOICE Mewing cry, 'peeioo'.
HABITAT AND DISTRIBUTION Moorland and agricultural land. Year-round resident across much of Europe. Declined dramatically in the 1950s and 60s, mainly because of the reduction in rabbit populations due to myxomatosis, and the introduction of organochlorine pesticides that reduced its ability to breed. Now fully protected; numbers have recovered with the increase in rabbit populations and withdrawl of harmful pesticides. Britain's most common bird of prey, with population totalling around 40,000 pairs.
FOOD AND HABITS Feeds mainly on small mammals, which it catches with a low-flying pounce; also carrion, birds, lizards and snakes, and large insects and earthworms when other prey is in short supply. May be seen flying overhead in gardens in rural areas. Nest is a bulky structure of twigs, usually erected in a tree.

KEY PREY SPECIES

European
Rabbit forms
a key part
of diet

Road-killed animals
such as Common
Pheasants are
common food items

Adult

Juvenile

Adults

Juvenile

Peregrine Falcon
Falco peregrinus

SIZE AND DESCRIPTION Length 45cm. Large and compact falcon with
a heavy build and broad pointed wings. Adults have strong black
moustaches and horizontal barring on the underparts, and are bluish
steely-grey above. Female larger than male (called the 'tiercel'). Chicks,
or 'eyases', have disproportionately large feet. Largest British falcon.

VOICE Calls are 'kee-kee-kee'.

HABITAT AND DISTRIBUTION Cliffs, mountains, and urban and open areas
throughout Europe. The species became endangered in the 1950s–60s
in many areas due to the use of organochlorine pesticides. It has been
recovering since their restriction.

FOOD AND HABITS Feeds on birds, including feral pigeons, which
comprise about 80 per cent of the diet in some cities. Occasionally
seen flying overhead in gardens. Circles high up waiting for prey to
fly below, then plunges at speeds of up to 325km/h in pursuit. Eggs
are laid in bare scrapes on cliff ledges, and increasingly on the tops of
tall buildings in towns and cities, which closely replicate the species'
natural nesting sites.

**Adult with
fledglings**

Adult

Juvenile

Adults

Juvenile

Hobby
Falco subbuteo

SIZE AND DESCRIPTION Length 32cm. Dashing slim little falcon that looks like a large swift in flight. Dark slaty-grey above with dark moustaches on white cheeks and throat, and red thighs.

VOICE A repeated clear 'kew-kew-kew'.

HABITAT AND DISTRIBUTION Open country such as farmland and marshes, and lowlands with scattered small woods. Summer visitor to Britain, wintering in Africa.

FOOD AND HABITS Feeds mainly on small birds, and large insects such as dragonflies, which are often eaten in flight. May be seen flying over gardens, and occasionally hunts in large rural gardens. Usually nests in an abandoned crow's nest, most often on the edge of a spinney or in a hedge.

Adult with fledglings

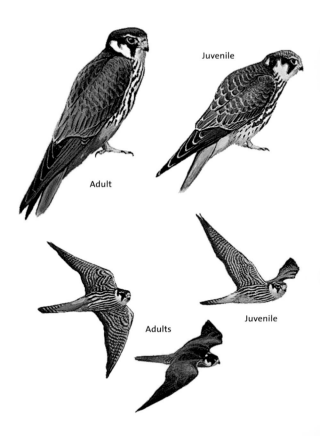

Juvenile

Adult

Adults

Juvenile

Kestrel
Falco tinnunculus

SIZE AND DESCRIPTION Length 34cm. Distinctive long tail and pointed wings. Male has a grey head, black-tipped grey tail and dark-flecked russet back. Female and juvenile lack the grey head, and have a brown tail with narrow bars, and more dark flecks on the back.

VOICE Noisy at nest-site; rasping 'kee-kee-kee-kee' call.

HABITAT AND DISTRIBUTION Farmland, moorland and other open areas. Breeds in cities and towns. Resident across Europe; northern and eastern European populations migrate during autumn.

FOOD AND HABITS Hovers above grassland or perches on trees and pylons, ready to drop down on rodents in grass. Also feeds on small birds, large insects and lizards. May visit bird tables for fat and meat scraps. Sometimes seen flying over gardens. Lays eggs in a hole or on a bare ledge, including on buildings.

Female on rooftop

Male

Female

Male

Female

Moorhen
Gallinula chloropus

SIZE AND DESCRIPTION Length 30cm. Distinctive slaty plumage, dark brown wings, white undertail coverts, yellow-tipped red bill and green legs with large, long-toed feet, typical of rails. Flicks tail as it walks with a careful tread. Juvenile is brown.

VOICE Varied repertoire includes harsh metallic 'krrek' and 'kittick' calls.

HABITAT AND DISTRIBUTION Ponds, rivers, canals, lakes and marshes across Europe. Also parks and gardens with large ponds.

FOOD AND HABITS Feeds on seeds, insects, molluscs, leaves and carrion. Nest is a bulky mound of vegetation on the water. Juveniles may help parents raise the next generation.

Juvenile

Adult

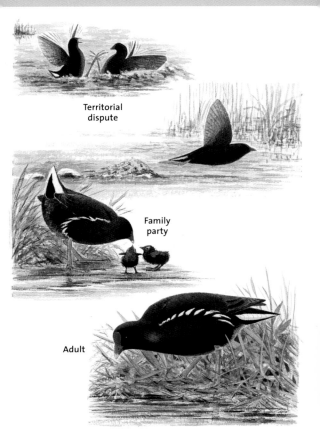

Territorial
dispute

Family
party

Adult

Coot
Fulica atra

SIZE AND DESCRIPTION Length 38cm. Mainly black water bird with a white bill and shield on the forehead, greenish feet and a domed back. Chicks are black with rufous heads. Juvenile is greyish.

VOICE Quite noisy; call usually a loud 'kowk' or variation.

HABITAT AND DISTRIBUTION Still and slow-moving fresh water. Usually found on larger and more open water bodies than Moorhen (page 58).

FOOD AND HABITS Dives for food, largely aquatic plants. May be seen in gardens with large ponds or streams, particularly those surrounded by dense vegetation. Often in flocks, especially outside the breeding season. Requires fringing vegetation for nesting. Quarrelsome; fights on the water using its large feet, especially during the breeding season, when it will attack birds much larger than itself such as swans and geese.

Juvenile

Adult

Large, distinctive feet, characteristic of rails

Chicks

Gathers in flocks outside breeding season

Common Gull
Larus canus

SIZE AND DESCRIPTION Length 41cm. Legs are yellow-green and the bill lacks a red spot. Grey upperparts, white below, black wingtips and a 'kinder' facial expression than that of many other gulls. Juvenile is streaked brown. Often in company with Black-headed Gulls (page 64).
VOICE Higher pitched than that of large gulls.
HABITAT AND DISTRIBUTION Coasts; breeds on moorland and freshwater lochs. Mainly resident in Britain, with winter visitors from northern Europe. After breeding many birds move south.
FOOD AND HABITS Feeds on earthworms, insects, seeds, small mammals, birds and marine invertebrates. May visit gardens in winter. Nest is a grassy cup on the ground.

First winter

Adult winter

First
winter

Second
winter

Adult winter

Adults summer

Black-headed Gull
Chroicocephalus ridibundus

SIZE AND DESCRIPTION Length 37cm. In winter the head is white with a grey-brown crescent behind the eye. Breeding birds have a chocolate-brown head. Bill is red and finer than the bills of most other European gulls.
VOICE Noisy when in flocks. Calls include a strident 'kee-yah'.
HABITAT AND DISTRIBUTION Breeds in colonies on moorland bogs, freshwater marshes and lakes, and in reed beds across northern Europe. In winter common on ploughed fields and coasts, and in town parks, playing fields and large gardens.
FOOD AND HABITS Feeds on seeds and invertebrates, and scavenges in rubbish. Noisy gangs of gulls sometimes visit bird tables in winter. Their presence may deter smaller birds from feeding. Nest is a large mound of flotsam and grass erected on the ground.

At bird table in winter

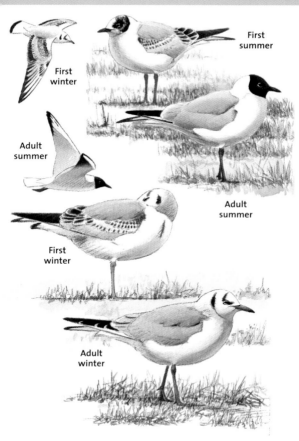

First
winter

First
summer

Adult
summer

Adult
summer

First
winter

Adult
winter

Stock Dove
Columba oenas

SIZE AND DESCRIPTION Length 30cm. Smaller and less chunky than
Woodpigeon (page 68), with no white on the neck or in the wings.
Noticeable black trailing edge to black-tipped wings. Lacks the
wingbars and white rump of feral pigeons.
VOICE A monotonously repeated 'roo-roo-oo'.
HABITAT AND DISTRIBUTION Woods and farmland, parks and gardens.
Breeds across Europe. Absent from Iceland.
FOOD AND HABITS Feeds on seeds and grain, often in flocks with
Woodpigeons. Unlikely to visit bird tables, but feeds on
garden plants and
spilt seeds. Nests
in a hollow tree
or burrow.

Adults

Adults

Nests in natural tree holes

Woodpigeon
Columba palumbus

SIZE AND DESCRIPTION Length 41cm. Largest European pigeon. Adult has white rings around the neck, and a white bar across each wing.
VOICE A soft, often repeated 'coo-coo-coo-cu-coo'.
HABITAT AND DISTRIBUTION Woodland, farmland, parks and gardens throughout Europe.
FOOD AND HABITS Eats seeds, berries and beechmast. Feeds in flocks throughout winter. Clumsy at bird tables, preferring to eat on the ground. Wings make a clattering sound on take-off and landing. Display flight, taking place February–March, involves a steep climb with clapping wings, and a glide down with tail spread. Nest is a platform of twigs in a tree or bush.

Adults

Display flight

Juvenile

Adults feeding on ground

Feral Pigeon
Columba livia var. *domestica*

SIZE AND DESCRIPTION Length 33cm. With black wingbars and a white rump, many feral pigeons resemble the now rare Rock Doves (*C. livia*) from which they originate. However, interbreeding with lost homing pigeons has resulted in a wide variety of plumage colours, ranging from white through very dark grey to pale fawn.

VOICE A soft cooing.

HABITAT AND DISTRIBUTION Common pigeon of Europe's town and city streets, where it breeds on buildings.

FOOD AND HABITS Feeds on seeds, grain and discarded human food. Nests in hollows and crevices of buildings.

Adults

Flocks are a common
sight in urban areas

Adults, showing
variations in colour

Collared Dove
Streptopelia decaocto

SIZE AND DESCRIPTION Length 32cm. Slimmer than other pigeons. Back is brown-buff, head and underparts pinkish-brown. Black ring around the nape of the neck, and wings with whitish undersides. Juvenile lacks the collar of the adult, and has a greyer, more scaly-looking plumage.
VOICE A rapidly repeated 'koo-koo, koo'.
HABITAT AND DISTRIBUTION Towns, gardens and farmland with hedges. Has spread across Europe from Asia since the 1950s.
FOOD AND HABITS Feeds on seeds, grain and fruits. Frequent bird-table visitor. Large flocks assemble at grain stores. Often perches on roadside wires, roofs and chimneys. Pairs for life and commonly seen in couples. Nest is a platform of twigs in a tree or bush, or on a ledge.

Adults often seen in pairs

Adults

Adult

Juvenile

Turtle Dove
Streptopelia turtur

SIZE AND DESCRIPTION Length 26cm. Adult rich bronze with the back and wings mottled with brown and black. Underparts pinkish-buff shading to white on the belly. Head and neck grey with chequered black-and-white collar patches. Juvenile has more subdued colouring than adult and no neck bars.

VOICE Distinctive gentle purring, 'turrr, turrr', from which the common name of the species is derived.

Adults

HABITAT AND DISTRIBUTION Woodland and farmland with hedges and scrub. Breeds over much of Europe except the far north. Winters in tropical Africa. European population has declined substantially, partly because of changing farming practices resulting in a scarcity of the plants on which it feeds, and partly due to the shooting of migrating birds in the Mediterranean.

FOOD AND HABITS Feeds mainly on the seeds of wild plants. Unlikely to visit bird tables, but may be attracted to large gardens with mature trees and shrubs. Nest is a platform of twigs in a bush.

Adults

Juvenile

Cuckoo
Cuculus canorus

SIZE AND DESCRIPTION Length 34cm. Slim-looking bird with long, swept-back wings and a long, rounded tail. Predominantly grey with a pale, barred breast; a small proportion of females are rufous-brown. Distinctive flight silhouette, with pointed wings and a long tail.

VOICE Males gives the well-known 'cuckoo' call, female a bubbling trill.

HABITAT AND DISTRIBUTION Wide range of habitats, including moorland, heathland, open woodland, parks and large gardens. Summer visitor to Europe from Africa, arriving in spring and leaving in summer.

FOOD AND HABITS Feeds on insects. Unique among British birds with its habit of parasitism on other birds, laying a single egg in a host's nest. The host birds then raise the chick, which is often several times their size. Various species of bird are targeted.

Long-eared Owl
Asio otus

Adults

Size and description Length
34cm. Cryptic brown
plumage, long ear-tufts
usually flattened in flight
and an orange iris.
Underparts are densely
streaked, and the wingtips
and tail are finely barred.
Voice Long low hoot during
the breeding season; juvenile utters a high-pitched 'squeaky gate' call.
Habitat and distribution Breeds mainly in coniferous forests across
Europe. In Britain uncommon and local.
Food and habits Feeds mainly on small mammals and birds, hunting
over open country from late dusk to early dawn. Occasional visitor to
large rural gardens with mature trees and scrub. Roosts communally
in thickets during winter. Nests almost exclusively in old crows' or
herons' nests, in secluded woodland sites.

Tawny Owl
Strix aluco

SIZE AND DESCRIPTION Length 38cm. Woodland owl more likely to be heard than seen as it is almost entirely nocturnal. Reddish-brown plumage, broad rounded wings, feathered feet, dark eyes and a round face mask. Grey-brown birds are rarely seen in Britain.

VOICE Song consists of familiar hooting, 'hooh, hu-huhu hooh'; call a sharp 'kewick'.

HABITAT AND DISTRIBUTION Deciduous woodland, forests and parks with mature trees across Europe except the north and Ireland.

FOOD AND HABITS Mostly eats small mammals such as Wood Mice, and small birds. Usually nests in holes in trees, but also in old crows' nests and even rabbit holes. May nest in nest boxes in large rural gardens (page 36).

Adult

Grey morph

Adult

Juveniles

Little Owl
Athene noctua

SIZE AND DESCRIPTION Length 22cm. More likely to be seen in daylight than other owls. Yellow eyes, a 'fierce' expression, long legs and brown upperparts spotted with white. Flight is a fast flap and glide.

VOICE Call a ringing 'kiew, kiew'.

HABITAT AND DISTRIBUTION Open country and farmland with scattered trees, and open woodland. An introduced species now widespread in much of Europe, including Britain, except the north and north-west.

FOOD AND HABITS Diet is chiefly large insects, especially beetles, and other invertebrates such as worms. Will run on the ground after prey. Rare in gardens, but may be seen in large rural gardens with nearby open country. Nests in holes in trees.

Adults

Undulating flight

Juvenile

Pursuing prey on ground

Barn Owl
Tyto alba

SIZE AND DESCRIPTION Length 34cm. Golden-spangled back, distinctive, heart-shaped whitish face and white underparts. Longer wings and legs than Tawny Owl's (page 78). North-east European Dark-breasted race *T. a. guttata*, an occasional visitor to Britain, is darker on the upperparts than the White-breasted western European race *T. a. alba*; it has a washed grey-brown face and rich buffy-brown underparts.

VOICE Call is a screech; also makes hissing and snoring sounds.

HABITAT AND DISTRIBUTION Fields, meadows and marshes; needs open country with rough grassland for hunting.

FOOD AND HABITS Feeds mainly on rodents, especially rats and voles. Often nests in buildings, usually old barns and farm outhouses. May use nest boxes in large rural gardens (page 38). Ghostly, buoyant flight; when pouncing on prey the wings are held straight up and the feet and head are held forwards. Largely nocturnal, and often seen in car headlights as it searches verges for prey.

'Mantling' with wings
to protect food

Chicks

Hunting flight and pounce

Adult White-breasted

Adult Dark-breasted

Kingfisher
Alcedo atthis

SIZE AND DESCRIPTION Length 18cm. Although brightly coloured and distinctive, Kingfishers are well camouflaged when perched among leaves. Bill is black, but female has a reddish base to the lower mandible. Juvenile has a pale spot at the tip of its bill.

VOICE Distinctive whistle, 'tee-eee' and 'tsee'.

HABITAT AND DISTRIBUTION Rivers, streams and lakes.

FOOD AND HABITS Fish are the main food. Hunts by diving into water from a perch, or by hovering, then diving. Rare in gardens, but may be seen in large gardens containing or near to streams. Excavates breeding tunnels in steep sandbanks.

Male

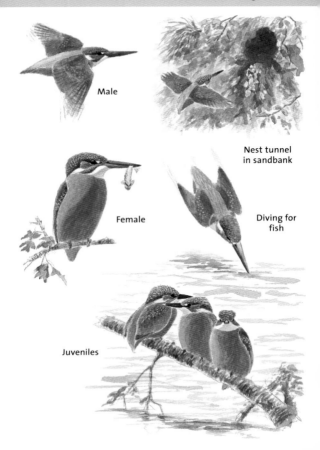

Male

Nest tunnel in sandbank

Female

Diving for fish

Juveniles

Green Woodpecker
Picus viridis

SIZE AND DESCRIPTION Length 33cm. Green plumage, but with a distinctive yellow rump and a red cap. A pale eye and black face and moustachial stripe give the bird a 'fierce' appearance. Male has a red centre to his moustachial stripe, while female's is black. Juvenile is speckled and appears more grey. Flight is deeply undulating.

VOICE An unmistakable shrill laughing call, hence its colloquial name of 'yaffle'. Rarely drums.

HABITAT AND DISTRIBUTION Deciduous and mixed forest edges, woodland, farmland, parkland and large gardens.

FOOD AND HABITS Feeds on insect grubs and ants, for which it probes soil and rotten wood with its long sticky tongue. Climbs trees with jerky hops. Eats up to 2,000 ants a day, hunting them on lawns. Often seen feeding on large open areas of grass. Nests in a hole made in a tree.

**Often probes for
ants on lawns**

Juvenile

Undulating flight

Female

Male

Great Spotted Woodpecker
Dendrocopos major

SIZE AND DESCRIPTION Length 24cm. A Blackbird-sized bird with white shoulder patches and red under the tail. Male has a red patch on the nape. Juvenile has a red crown. Shows distinctive oval patches on the wings in flight, which is undulating.

VOICE A short, sharp 'tchak' call, which may be repeated at 1-second intervals. In spring drums very fast on rotten branches.

HABITAT AND DISTRIBUTION All kinds of woodland, large gardens and parks.

FOOD AND HABITS Eats insects and grubs, and conifer seeds in winter. Visits garden feeders, especially for nuts in winter, usually displacing other, smaller birds due to its larger size. Also steals eggs and young from other birds' nests. Nests in a hole made in a tree.

Male

Female

Male

Juvenile

Lesser Spotted Woodpecker
Dendrocopos minor

SIZE AND DESCRIPTION Length 26cm. Miniature version of Great Spotted Woodpecker (page 88), the size of a House Sparrow (page 164). Fine white barring on the back. Undulating flight.

VOICE Longer and more high-pitched drumming than that of Great.

HABITAT AND DISTRIBUTION Lives in deciduous forests, often close to wetlands. In Britain occurs in southern England and Wales, and is declining. (All woodpecker species are absent from Ireland.)

FOOD AND HABITS Feeds mainly on insects, particularly grubs and beetles that live in wood. Rarely visits bird tables, though it will take seeds in gardens.

Nests in a tree hole

Male

Female

Juvenile

Male

Common Swift
Apus apus

SIZE AND DESCRIPTION Length 17cm. Long and narrow, crescent-shaped wings, a torpedo-shaped body, a short forked tail and very short legs. Plumage is dark brown with a pale throat.

VOICE Shrill monotone scream, often uttered by tight flocks flying around buildings.

HABITAT AND DISTRIBUTION Breeds in towns and villages, but feeds in the sky, often several kilometres from nest sites. Summer visitor to northern Europe (except Iceland), usually arriving in May and leaving in August.

FOOD AND HABITS Adapted to feed on high-flying insects, which it catches in its wide gaping mouth. Shuffles around its nest site on short legs. Most of its life is spent on the wing, and parties of screaming swifts flying over the rooftops of towns and villages are a familiar sight during summer.

Typical summertime flight in screaming parties

Juvenile

Adults

Swallow
Hirundo rustica

SIZE AND DESCRIPTION Length 19cm, including tail of 3–6.5cm. Wings long and pointed, tail deeply forked and longer in male than in female. Pale cream underparts, dark blue wings and back, and a red throat with a blue-black neck band. Fast flight with powerful wingbeats.

VOICE High-pitched 'vit-vit' call in flight. Warning call for cats and other ground predators a sharp 'sifflit'; for birds of prey, 'flitt-flitt'. Song a rapid rattling twitter.

Often congregates on telegraph wires

Juvenile

HABITAT AND DISTRIBUTION Breeds in farmyards and small-village gardens
with surrounding open country. Often seen near water. Summer
visitor to northern Europe.

FOOD AND HABITS Feeds on insects, which it catches in flight by flying
low over fields and water. Congregates on telegraph wires, TV aerials
and roadside wires in autumn, in preparation for the journey south
of the Sahara. Cup-shaped clay nest is built in buildings and may be
returned to year after year. May use an artificial next box (page 34)
for nesting.

Adults

Female

Male

House Martin
Delichon urbica

SIZE AND DESCRIPTION Length 14cm. Wings broader than Swallow's (page 94) and forked tail shorter, giving a stubbier appearance. Rump white, and wings, head and tail dark blue. Underparts of juvenile usually duskier white than adult's. Flight more fluttery than Swallow's, with flaps often interspersed with glides.

VOICE Harsh twitter. Song a series of formless chirps.

HABITAT AND DISTRIBUTION Breeds in colonies in towns and villages, and on cliffs. Summer visitor and migrant across Europe except the far north. Winters in Africa.

FOOD AND HABITS Tends to feed on flying insects at greater altitude than Swallow. Rarely on the ground, except when collecting mud for nest. Builds a rounded mud nest on the eaves of buildings, and sometimes cliffs, which were the traditional nest sites. Gregarious, and may even nest near other species. May use a specially constructed House Martin box fixed under the eaves of a building (page 34) for nesting.

Collecting mud
for nest

Flight over buildings

Perching

Nesting with House Sparrows

Skylark
Alauda arvensis

Head, showing
erect crest

Song
flight

Adult winter

Adult summer

SIZE AND DESCRIPTION
Length 18cm. Streaked
brown upperparts, not
always obvious short
crest and white outer tail feathers. Walks rather
than hops. Towering and hovering song flight.

VOICE Lengthy warbling song delivered in flight as the bird rises
vertically, then drops through the air.

HABITAT AND DISTRIBUTION Farmland, grassland, meadows and moorland
throughout most of Europe. Common but declining.

FOOD AND HABITS Eats insects, worms and seeds. Flocks in winter, when
numbers are swollen by European migrants. May be seen around
large rural gardens, mostly flying overhead. Nest a grassy cup well
hidden on the ground.

Meadow Pipit
Anthus pratensis

Male song flight

Adult winter

Adult summer

SIZE AND DESCRIPTION Length 15cm. Streaked brown upperparts; underparts spotted. Similar to Skylark (opposite), but with a more slender beak and generally slimmer. Best identified by its call.
VOICE Call 'pheet', uttered 1–5 times. Song given from a perch or in a display flight as it describes an arc from the ground.
HABITAT AND DISTRIBUTION Open country, heathland, moorland and grassland. May be seen in lowlands or on coastal land in winter. Year-round resident, migrant or winter visitor in much of Europe.
FOOD AND HABITS Eats mostly insects; also spiders, earthworms and some seeds. In gardens, mostly seen flying overhead. Nests on the ground in a small depression.

Grey Wagtail
Motacilla cinerea

SIZE AND DESCRIPTION Length 19cm. Longest tailed of European wagtails. Grey above and lemon yellow below, with colour particularly strong under the tail, and pink legs. Summer adult male has a distinctive black throat. Tail is constantly wagging.

VOICE Call a sharp 'tzit'. Song a simple and metallic 'ziss-ziss-ziss'.

HABITAT AND DISTRIBUTION Vicinity of running water, from mountain streams to towns. Found around lakes, ponds and even city centres. Occurs year-round throughout much of Europe; summer visitor to the north and north-east.

FOOD AND HABITS Insectivorous; often chases insects over the water. May be seen around ponds outside the breeding season. Nest is a grassy cup usually hidden in a cavity near water.

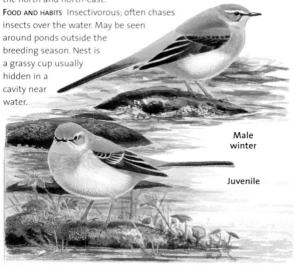

Male winter

Juvenile

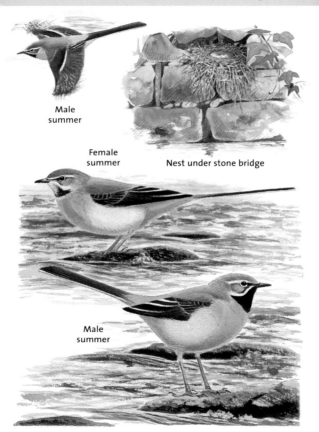

Male summer

Female summer

Nest under stone bridge

Male summer

Pied & White Wagtails
Motacilla alba

SIZE AND DESCRIPTION Length 18cm. Male of British race Pied Wagtail
(*M. a. yarrellii*) has a black back and wings, female a dark grey back.
In continental race White Wagtail (*M. a. alba*), both male and female
have a pale grey back. In flight, which is undulating, faint double
wingbars can be seen.

VOICE Flight call a 'chissick', sometimes a 'chissick-ick'. Song twittery.

HABITAT AND DISTRIBUTION Towns, gardens and open habitats.

FOOD AND HABITS Runs rapidly after flying insects. Will also take worms
and seeds, and pick up bits underneath bird tables. On the ground its
gait is rapid, and its head is moved
backwards and forwards while wagging
its tail. Prefers feeding on lawns and
roofs, and in car parks and roads,
where prey is easily spotted. In
winter roosts in large flocks in
warm places like factories.
Nest is a grassy cup in a cavity.

Male Pied

Female
Pied

Pied

Adult White

First winter male Pied

Juvenile Pied

Waxwing
Bombycilla garrulus

Size and description Length 20cm. Starling-sized bird with overall pinkish-brown plumage, a long crest, black chin and mask, and yellow-banded tail. Male usually brighter in colour than female. Waxy red tips on the ends of the secondary feathers are quite marked, and give the bird its common name. Juveniles have a shorter crest, browner plumage and less yellow on the tail than adults; the waxy red colour on the secondaries is nearly always missing.

Voice Call a soft sibilant trilling, 'sirrrr'. Song a slow and soft, bell-like trill with rougher notes.

Habitat and distribution In Europe breeds in the far northern taiga with coniferous forests. In winter flocks to parks and gardens where there are berries south to Britain and the Balkans.

Food and habits Feeds mainly on berries, supplemented by insects, particularly during the breeding season. In Britain, flocks of Waxwings often gorge themselves on berry bushes before moving on.

Flying near berry bushes

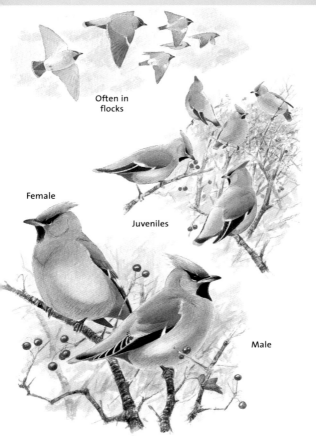

Often in flocks

Female

Juveniles

Male

Wren
Troglodytes troglodytes

SIZE AND DESCRIPTION Length 10cm. Tiny bird with a short tail often held cocked above the back, a round body and a short neck. Reddish-brown back is faintly barred, as are the paler flanks. Narrow dark eyestripe and paler stripe above the eye. Whirring flight, rather like that of a large bee.

VOICE Calls a repeated 'tic-tic' and metallic 'clink'. Song an amazingly loud series of alternately sweet and rattling trills and warbles.

HABITAT AND DISTRIBUTION Woodland with dense undergrowth, scrub, heathland, gardens, parks and moorland in most of Europe.

FOOD AND HABITS Searches mouse-like for insects and spiders on or near the ground. May visit bird tables to pick up small morsels of food such as crumbs and grated cheese. Normally fiercely territorial, due to its small size it can have difficulty surviving cold winter nights; flocks may roost together for warmth crammed into a cavity, including nest boxes. Nest is a domed grassy structure well hidden in a hollow or vegetation. Males may build more than one nest for females to select from.

Family group of newly fledged Wrens

Nesting

Over 60 Wrens have been reported in a nest box in winter

Singing male

Dunnock
Prunella modularis

SIZE AND DESCRIPTION Length 14cm. Streaking and brown colouration give this bird a rather sparrow-like appearance, which is why it is often described as a Hedge Sparrow. It has a thin, insect-picking bill, grey throat and face, and reddish-brown legs.

VOICE Alarm call a strong 'tiih'. Song clear and quite loud.

HABITAT AND DISTRIBUTION Gardens, parks, open woodland, heathland, farmland and hedges over most of Europe.

FOOD AND HABITS An unobtrusive bird that scurries around on the ground, mouse-like, looking for seeds, berries, insects and other invertebrates. Takes fruits and scraps that fall from bird tables and feeders, but rarely sits on bird tables. In late winter and spring, males enter a display involving flicking each wing in turn for several minutes, with one male often drawing others to an area. Nest is a grass cup well hidden in a shrub.

Adult

Singing

Male display

Juvenile

Blackbird
Turdus merula

SIZE AND DESCRIPTION Length 25cm. All-black adult male, with his yellow bill and yellow eyering, is unmistakable. Sooty-brown female, with a dark-streaked pale throat, and the gingery juvenile, may be confused with other thrushes, but they have a solid build and cock their tails when landing. First-winter males have all-dark bills.

Singing on rooftop

Female

Male

VOICE Alarm call a harsh 'chack-aack-aack-aack', or a series of high metallic notes when going to roost or when a cat is seen. Song a rich melodic fluting, often rising to a crescendo.

HABITAT AND DISTRIBUTION Woodland, parks, orchards and gardens throughout Europe.

FOOD AND HABITS Hops or walks over the ground, stopping and cocking its head to look for worms or other food. Eats a wide range of foods, including insects, worms, fruits and berries. Takes food from bird tables, and adults also bring fledglings to tables – avoid offering large food morsels such as cat or dog biscuits, which can choke young birds.

Pulling worm from ground

Juvenile

Fieldfare
Turdus pilaris

SIZE AND DESCRIPTION Length 26cm. Smaller than Mistle Thrush (page 118), but looks stockier. Grey head, red-brown back and apricot base to the speckled breast. Longish tail, pale grey rump and white underwings show clearly in the rather flapping flight.

VOICE Call a dry 'chack-chack-chack', like that of a Magpie (page 154). Song a tuneless chattering babble.

HABITAT AND DISTRIBUTION Open forest, town parks, fields and gardens. Winter visitor or migrant to much of Europe; year-round in north-central areas; summer only in the far north. In Britain breeds rarely in Scotland.

FOOD AND HABITS On arrival mainly from Scandinavia, initially feeds on berries and fruits, particularly from hawthorns; later takes worms and insects in open fields, often with other thrushes such as Redwings (page 114). Fond of windfall fruits, and may visit gardens to feed on them. Nest is a grassy cup in the fork of a tree.

Feeding on windfall apples with other thrushes

Winter flock in open countryside

Juvenile

Male

Female

Redwing
Turdus iliacus

SIZE AND DESCRIPTION Length 21cm. Similar size to Song Thrush (page 116), but with a larger head. White stripe above the eye and black-tipped yellow bill give it a striking appearance. Red patch under the wing conspicuous in flight, which is fast and direct. Juvenile basically the same as adult, except for the white or buffy tips to the greater coverts of the wings.

VOICE Thin 'tseep' contact call. Alarm call hoarse and scolding. Song variable, with loud fluted notes and prolonged twitters.

Adult

HABITAT AND DISTRIBUTION Fields, open woodland, parks and gardens. Summer visitor to northern Europe, wintering in southern and western Europe.

FOOD AND HABITS Feeds on berries, worms and insects. Feeding habits on its British wintering grounds much the same as for Fieldfare (page 112). Smaller and shyer than other thrushes. Visits gardens only in the harshest weather to raid berry bushes and windfall fruits. Nest is a grassy cup in a shrub or tree.

Flight

Feeding on ground with Song Thrush

Juvenile

Song Thrush
Turdus philomelos

SIZE AND DESCRIPTION Length 23cm. Brown back and speckled creamy breast. Speckles shaped like arrowheads, and more regular than those of Mistle Thrush (page 118). In flight, the underwings show yellowish-orange. Juvenile similar to adult, but with paler marks on the mantle, smaller spots on the underside and a more buffy wash to the underparts. Flies rather jerkily.

VOICE Beautiful strong song with a variety of trilling and squeaky notes and frequent repetitions, often sung at dusk. Alarm call a series of sharp scolding notes.

HABITAT AND DISTRIBUTION Woodland, parks and gardens across most of Europe. Common but declining.

FOOD AND HABITS Feeds on worms, insects, berries and snails. May dash snails against a hard anvil, such as a stone or tree root, to break open the shells. Sometimes in small flocks. Does not use bird tables, but may take scraps below them and birdfeeders; sultanas are a favourite food. Nest is a mud-lined grassy cup low down in thick foliage.

Nesting

Adult

Juvenile

Breaking open
snail shell

Adult

Mistle Thrush
Turdus viscivorus

SIZE AND DESCRIPTION Length 28cm. Large thrush with a comparatively longer tail than that of Song Thrush (page 116). White breast speckled with rounded blotchy spots. In flight white outer tail feathers and narrow white wingbars can be seen. Underwing is white. Juvenile similar to adult but appears quite spotted and streaked on the entire underparts, and has a plainer face pattern, strongly marked wings and a strong pale yellowish-buff wash on the underparts. Stands in an upright posture. Flight more undulating than Song Thrush's.

Pulling worm from ground

Adult

Voice Flight call a dry churring rattle. Song similar to Song Thrush's.
Habitat and distribution Woodland, parks and gardens throughout Europe. Common but declining.
Food and habits Eats worms, berries and insects. Feeds alongside other birds. Larger and more aggressive than other thrushes, and will defend food sources from other birds. Visits bird tables in gardens, taking a variety of foods. Nest is an untidy grass and leaf cup usually high up in the tree canopy.

Adult

Adult singing

Juvenile

Goldcrest
Regulus regulus

Male displaying,
showing raised
crown feathers

Juvenile

Female

SIZE AND DESCRIPTION Length 9cm. Tiny with a greenish back and a
yellow crest that becomes orange in male. Crest has a black stripe on
each side. Face greyish with dark eyes surrounded by very pale grey.
Juvenile is a dull version of the adult, with no crown markings.
VOICE Very high-pitched, thin call of 3–4 syllables, 'see-see-see'. Song
high-pitched and rhythmic, and ending with a trill.
HABITAT AND DISTRIBUTION Coniferous and mixed woodland; often seen
in Yew and cypress trees.
FOOD AND HABITS Feeds on tiny insects and spiders on the undersides
of leaves. Also eats small seeds, and occasionally investigates
birdfeeders. Nest is a mossy hammock high in a tree.

Firecrest
Regulus ignicapilla

Juvenile

Male

Female

SIZE AND DESCRIPTION Length 9cm. Similar to Goldcrest (opposite).
In all plumages has a black eyestripe and white supercilium.
VOICE Call slightly lower pitched than Goldcrest's, rising in pitch
when notes are consecutive. Song very high-pitched and ascending,
'si si-sisisisihrr'.
HABITAT AND DISTRIBUTION Coniferous and mixed woodland and parks;
also more open bushy places in winter. Occurs in much of central
and western Europe. In Britain scarce and local.
FOOD AND HABITS Feeds on insects. Rare in gardens. Nest like that
of a Goldcrest.

Sedge Warbler
Acrocephalus schoenobaenus

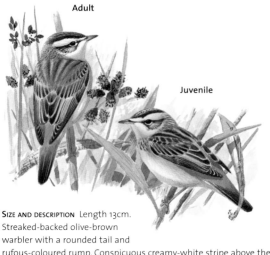

Adult

Juvenile

Size and description Length 13cm.
Streaked-backed olive-brown
warbler with a rounded tail and
rufous-coloured rump. Conspicuous creamy-white stripe above the
eye. Sexes look similar.

Voice Loud, jumbly and scratchy song.

Habitat and distribution Waterside vegetation near reed beds, rivers
and lakes, and lowland marshes; also dry scrubby areas. Summer
visitor to Britain, migrating to Africa in late summer.

Food and habits Mainly eats insects; takes berries in autumn. May be
seen in gardens that adjoin wetlands. Nests in rank vegetation.

Willow Warbler
Phylloscopus trochilus

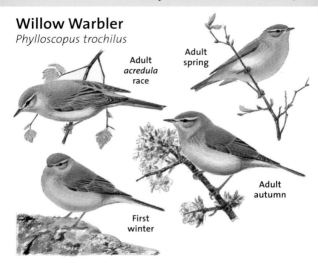

Adult *acredula* race

Adult spring

Adult autumn

First winter

SIZE AND DESCRIPTION Length 11.5cm. Head, back and tail generally brownish-green; throat and eyebrows yellowish; legs usually pale brown. Primary feathers project beyond tertials. Juvenile in autumn is particularly striking, with rich lemon-yellow underparts. Scandinavian race *P. t. acredula* is paler than central European race *P. t. trochilus*, with the head and upperparts a washed-out pale greenish colour.

VOICE Call a soft 'huitt' similar to Common Chiffchaff's (page 124). Song rather sad.

HABITAT AND DISTRIBUTION Upland birchwoods and other deciduous woods, and parks and large gardens. Occurs across much of Europe apart from the south.

FOOD AND HABITS Feeds on insects found among leaves. Nest is a grassy dome on or near the ground.

Common Chiffchaff
Phylloscopus collybita

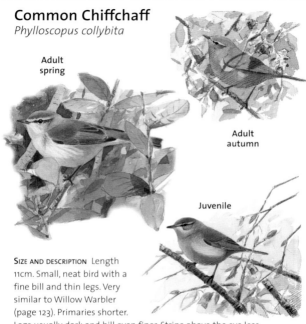

**Adult
spring**

**Adult
autumn**

Juvenile

SIZE AND DESCRIPTION Length
11cm. Small, neat bird with a
fine bill and thin legs. Very
similar to Willow Warbler
(page 123). Primaries shorter.
Legs usually dark and bill even finer. Stripe above the eye less
distinct, while the darkish patch beneath the eye emphasizes the
white eyering. Juvenile quite brightly marked, with rich olive-green
upperparts and washed yellow below.

VOICE Call a soft 'hueet'. Song a distinctively slow 'chiff-chaff-chiff-chaff'.

HABITAT AND DISTRIBUTION Open deciduous woodland with some scrub.
Mainly a summer visitor to Britain, Scandinavia and central Europe.

FOOD AND HABITS Similar to those of Willow Warbler.

Garden Warbler
Sylvia borin

Juvenile

Adult

SIZE AND DESCRIPTION Length 14cm. Inconspicuous little grey-brown warbler. Plumage uniform without any notable distinguishing feature. Round head and short bill.

VOICE Song the most distinctive characteristic, a musical warble uttered from the depths of cover.

HABITAT AND DISTRIBUTION Deciduous and mixed woodland with dense undergrowth. Summer visitor to Britain.

FOOD AND HABITS Eats mostly insects in early summer; also berries and other fruits before autumn migration. Not common in gardens, despite its name, and often confused with Common Chiffchaff and Willow Warbler. Often difficult to see due to its preference for dense cover, and best detected by its song. Nests in brambles and bushes.

Blackcap
Sylvia atricapilla

SIZE AND DESCRIPTION Length 14cm. Male has a black cap; female's cap is red-brown. Cheeks grey; upperparts dark grey-brown. Juvenile male's cap a mixture of brown and black.

VOICE Warning call a harsh 'teck' and 'tack'ack'ack'. Sweet, rich and warbling song.

HABITAT AND DISTRIBUTION Open woodland, shrubby areas with trees and gardens. Mostly a summer visitor to Britain; increasing numbers seen in winter.

FOOD AND HABITS Chiefly eats insects, and berries and fruits in late summer and autumn. Increasingly common in gardens, often feeding on berries in autumn. Occasional visitor to bird tables. Nest is a neat grass cup concealed low in a bush.

Often feeds on berries in autumn

Female

Male

Juvenile
male

Common Whitethroat
Sylvia communis

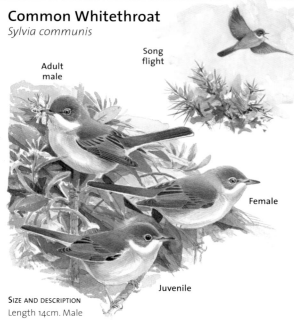

Song flight

Adult male

Female

Juvenile

SIZE AND DESCRIPTION
Length 14cm. Male
has a grey head, a bright white throat, brown upperparts and pale
underparts. Female has a brown head. Tail long and slim.

VOICE Call a sharp 'tacc, tacc'. Song a rapid, scratchy warble.

HABITAT AND DISTRIBUTION Open woodland, gardens, hedgerows and
scrub. Summer visitor to Britain.

FOOD AND HABITS Eats mainly insects, and some fruits and berries
in autumn. May visit rural gardens with bushes. Nests in brambles
and low bushes not far from the ground.

Lesser Whitethroat
Sylvia curruca

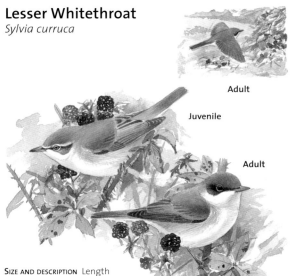

Adult

Juvenile

Adult

SIZE AND DESCRIPTION Length 13cm. Easy to distinguish from Common Whitethroat (opposite) by the duller brown back and wings, lacking any rufous colouration, bright white underparts and dark grey legs.

VOICE Call an abrupt 'tack'. Song a simple brief warble ending with a repetitive single-note rattle.

HABITAT AND DISTRIBUTION Farmland with trees and hedges, woodland edges, parks, large gardens and scrub. Summer visitor to Britain.

FOOD AND HABITS Insectivorous, but also takes berries and other soft fruits. Grass cup nest is built in a low shrub or brambles.

Spotted Flycatcher
Muscicapa striata

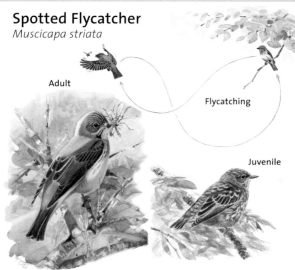

Adult

Flycatching

Juvenile

SIZE AND DESCRIPTION Length 14cm. Back greyish-brown with pale underparts; close examination reveals a streaked forehead and faintly streaked upper breast. Bill and legs black, and the black eye an obvious feature. Upright posture when perched.

VOICE Call a short shrill 'tzee'. Song quiet, simple and scratchy, often with soft trills.

HABITAT AND DISTRIBUTION Open woodland and gardens throughout Europe in summer. Winters in Africa.

FOOD AND HABITS Flies up from perch to snatch flying insects, then returns to the same spot. Visits large rural gardens that have plenty of flowering plants to attract insects. Breeds in hollows or dense vegetation. May use nest boxes (page 32).

Pied Flycatcher
Ficedula hypoleuca

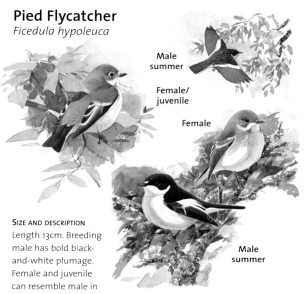

Male summer

Female/juvenile

Female

Male summer

SIZE AND DESCRIPTION

Length 13cm. Breeding male has bold black-and-white plumage. Female and juvenile can resemble male in autumn, brown above, whitish below. Shorter tailed and more compact than Spotted Flycatcher (opposite), with a white wingbar. Constantly flicks its wings and tail.

VOICE Calls include a metallic 'whit'. Song quite shrill, 'zee-it, zee-it', interspersed with trills.

HABITAT AND DISTRIBUTION Deciduous and sometimes coniferous forest. Summer visitor to Britain.

FOOD AND HABITS Feeds on insects caught on the wing, and sometimes on the ground. Seldom hunts from the same perch twice. Breeds in hollows and may use nest boxes (page 32).

Robin
Erithacus rubecula

SIZE AND DESCRIPTION Length 13cm. Familiar bird with an orange-red breast fringed with pale grey, and a pale wingbar. Juvenile has a pale-spotted brown breast, and a pale-flecked head and back.

VOICE Call a repeated short hard 'tic'; alarm call a thin, sharp 'tsiih'. Song sweet and silvery, starting high, then falling, then speeding up in clear notes.

HABITAT AND DISTRIBUTION Woodland bird that breeds in gardens, parks and forest edges. In winter, northern European Robins migrate south-west to southern Europe. Other populations are resident.

FOOD AND HABITS Feeds on berries and insects on the ground. Moves over the ground by hopping vigorously. Known for being pugnacious with others of its species and fearless of humans; may take worms from the hand, becoming skulking only when nesting. Nest is a grassy cup well hidden on or near the ground; it may be in a cavity.

Adult feeding juvenile

Adult

Juvenile

Employs a variety of postures, sometimes strutting, at other times inquisitive

Nesting

Black Redstart
Pheonicurus ochruros

Female

Male first
summer

Male
summer

SIZE AND DESCRIPTION Length 14cm. Darker than Common Redstart
(opposite). Breeding male slaty-black above with a black face and
breast, and a white flash in the wing. Female duller brown. Reddish
rump and tail, which it constantly shivers.

VOICE Call a quiet 'tsip-tsip'. Song a short, high-pitched warble
punctuated by characteristic gravelly notes.

HABITAT AND DISTRIBUTION Towns, urban sites and cliffs. Summer visitor
to northern Europe. Rare breeder in south-east England.

FOOD AND HABITS Eats mainly insects. Often nests in wall cavities.

Common Redstart
Phoenicurus phoenicurus

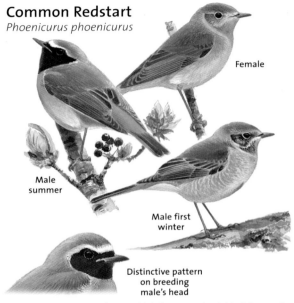

Female

Male
summer

Male first
winter

Distinctive pattern
on breeding
male's head

SIZE AND DESCRIPTION Length 14cm. Male has a grey back, black face and
throat, white forehead, and bright chestnut breast and tail. Female is
a duller brown. Tail is waved up and down.

VOICE Calls 'hooeet' and 'kwee-tucc-tucc'. Song a squeaky warble.

HABITAT AND DISTRIBUTION Usually deciduous upland woodland with
mature trees for nesting. Occurs in much of Europe in summer and
a common visitor to Britain. Winters in Africa.

FOOD AND HABITS Eats mainly insects; also worms, spiders and berries.
Nests in a tree hollow.

Long-tailed Tit
Aegithalos caudatus

SIZE AND DESCRIPTION Length 14cm, including tail that is at least as long as its dumpy body. With its pink, black and white body and long tail, this species is unmistakable. Juveniles have shorter tails than adults and are darker around the face, head and nape. Western European race (*A. c. rosaceus*) has dark crown stripes, but *A. c. caudatus* of north-east Europe has a pure white head.

VOICE Call a piercing 'tsee-tsee-tsee'. Song similar to Blue Tit's (page 138).

HABITAT AND DISTRIBUTION Woods with bushy undergrowth, hedges and gardens throughout most of Europe.

FOOD AND HABITS Feeds mainly on insects and small spiders, and is increasingly visiting birdfeeders. Families form into flocks and move through woods and hedges, often with other tits (page 18). Nest is ball-shaped and camouflaged with lichens, built in a branch fork.

Roosts communally in winter

Juveniles

Adults
rosaceus
race

Juvenile
rosaceus race

Northern
caudatus
race

Nest

Blue Tit
Cyanistes caeruleus

SIZE AND DESCRIPTION Length 12cm. Smaller than Great Tit (page 140) and with a bright blue crown. Stripe down the yellow breast less well-defined than Great Tit's. Tail and wings blue. Young birds have yellow cheeks, and green parts instead of the blue parts of adults.
VOICE Call a thin 'see-see'. Clear, ringing and high-pitched song.
HABITAT AND DISTRIBUTION Mixed and deciduous woodland, parks and gardens. Found across Europe except Iceland and northern Norway.
FOOD AND HABITS Feeds on insects, spiders and other small animals, finding them on tree branches and sometimes in the corners of windows. Frequently visits bird tables and birdfeeders in winter. Feeds in flocks of up to 30 in winter, often with other small bird species. Nests in holes in trees, buildings or banks.

Feeding at peanut feeder

In mixed flock
of small birds

Juveniles

Adults

Great Tit
Parus major

SIZE AND DESCRIPTION Length 14cm. A black cap and black stripe starting at the bill give this bird a more ferocious expression than a Blue Tit's (page 138). Male's breast-stripe becomes broader than female's. Juvenile much duller than either adult.

VOICE Rich and varied repertoire includes a metallic 'pink' and a repeated 'teacher-teacher'.

Adult feeding young

Male displaying

HABITAT AND DISTRIBUTION Woodlands and gardens across Europe except the far north. Many Great Tits feeding in gardens in winter return to woods to feed in spring.

FOOD AND HABITS Feeds on seeds and fruits; also spiders and insect larvae in the breeding season. Eats sunflower seeds, peanuts and fat at birdfeeders. Nest as Blue Tit's.

Female

Male

Juvenile

Coal Tit
Periparus ater

SIZE AND DESCRIPTION Length 11cm. Smaller than Great Tit (page 140) with a proportionately larger head. British race *P. a. britannicus* has a black head with white cheeks, and a white patch on the nape. Back grey and breast grey-brown. Irish race *P. a. hibernicus* has pale yellow on the cheeks, nape and underparts. Northern European *P. a. ater* has whiter cheeks than British race, a greyer back and paler buff-pink underparts.

Adult *hibernicus* race

Adult *ater* race

Juvenile

Voice Most frequent call a triple 'tsee-tsee-tsee'. Song like a simpler and weaker Great Tit's song.

Habitat and distribution Woodland and gardens across Europe except the far north. Prefers coniferous trees.

Food and habits Eats insects and seeds, particularly spruce cones in the north. Commonly visits gardens, where it is very partial to nuts. Nest as Blue Tit's (page 138).

Feeding at seed feeder

Adults
britannicus
race

Willow Tit
Poecile montanus

SIZE AND DESCRIPTION Length 12cm. Plumage similar to Marsh Tit's (page 146), especially in summer, but Willow has a heavier neck, duller black crown, slightly larger bib and sometimes a pale patch on the closed wing. Northern European race (*P. m. borealis*) is paler than British race (*P. m. kleinschmidti*), with a greyer mantle, wings and tail, and white cheeks and underparts.

VOICE Call variable, for example a low-pitched, nasal and down-slurred 'zur' or 'si-si-zur zur zur'. Song a melanchonic and bell-like 'tyu tyu tyu'.

HABITAT AND DISTRIBUTION Forests, scrub and parks in Europe apart from the south-west. In Britain resident in England, Wales and southern Scotland.

FOOD AND HABITS Feeds on insects, caterpillars and seeds. May visit birdfeeders. Nests in tree hollows, which it excavates itself.

Worn summer plumage

At nesthole

Adult *borealis* race

Adults *kleinschmidti* race

Marsh Tit
Poecile palustris

Adult *palustris* race

Adult *dresseri* race

At nesthole

SIZE AND DESCRIPTION Length 12cm. Very similar to Willow Tit (page 144), with a large-headed and short-tailed appearance, but with a shiny black cap, smaller black bib and uniform wings. Northern European race (*P. p. palustris*) is paler than British race (*P. p. dresseri*).

VOICE Best distinguishing feature is the call, 'pitchiuu'. Song a liquid bubbling sound.

HABITAT AND DISTRIBUTION Mainly deciduous woodland, and sometimes gardens, across much of central and western Europe.

FOOD AND HABITS Diet mainly insects, with seeds, berries and beechmast, like other tits. Favours gardens adjoining woodland, and visits birdfeeders. Nests in tree holes, especially in alders and willows, which it does not excavate itself, preferring to use natural cavities.

Crested Tit
Lophophanes cristatus

Characteristic tit posture

Adult

Size and description Length 12cm. Distinctive chequered black-and-white head with a pointed crest. Upperparts are grey-brown, underparts buff-toned.

Voice Most frequently a buzzing 'buurrrret'.

Habitat and distribution In Britain restricted in both range and habitat, breeding only in mature pine forests in the Scottish Highlands.

Food and habits Frequently seen in pine trees searching for food. In places where it is found it is quite tame and often visits garden birdfeeders, particularly in winter.

Nuthatch
Sitta europaea

SIZE AND DESCRIPTION Length 14cm. Large head, no neck, short tail and heavy pointed bill. Back and head slate-grey with a long black eyestripe. Cheeks white, and breast and underparts in western European race *S. e. caesia* rusty orange (darker in male). Northern European *S. e. europea* race is white below. Flight similar to a woodpecker's, but tail is rounded.

VOICE A loud strident 'hwitt' call. Song a repetitive 'peeu-peeu-peeu'.

HABITAT AND DISTRIBUTION Mixed deciduous woods, parks and gardens with mature oaks from western Russia across Europe; absent from Ireland and Scotland.

FOOD AND HABITS Feeds on nuts, seeds and invertebrates, using its bill to winkle insects out of bark crevices. Frequent visitor to birdfeeders, where it can be quite dominant. In gardens it will eat peanuts, sunflower seeds, bird cake and fatty mixtures smeared on tree trunks. Caches food such as seed and nuts, sometimes hoarding it for several months before retrieval. Nests in a cavity, usually in a tree, with the entrance plastered with mud to provide the correct size.

Nesting hole in tree – entrance plastered with mud

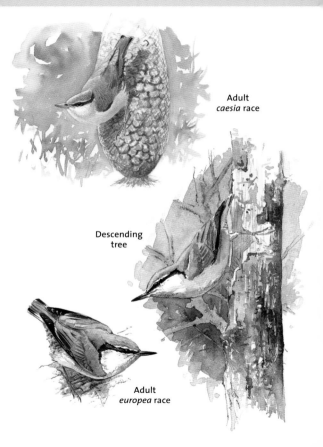

Adult
caesia race

Descending
tree

Adult
europea race

Treecreeper
Certhia familiaris

SIZE AND DESCRIPTION Length 13cm. Mottled brown on the back and white on the underside, providing excellent camouflage against tree trunks. Fine bill curves downwards. Long stiff tail helps the bird balance in an upright position against a trunk.

VOICE Call a loud and thin 'zzrreet'. Song is several scratchy notes ending in a thin trill.

HABITAT AND DISTRIBUTION Almost all woodland, parks, gardens and orchards with old trees that have loose bark for nest-sites. Occurs throughout Europe except the south.

FOOD AND HABITS Probes bark crevices for insects and small spiders. Moves on a tree by flying to the bottom and hopping with both feet in a spiral path up and around the trunk, before flying to the bottom of the next tree. Often roams with tit flocks in winter (page 18). Nests in a crevice behind a flap of bark, and may use nest boxes (page 35).

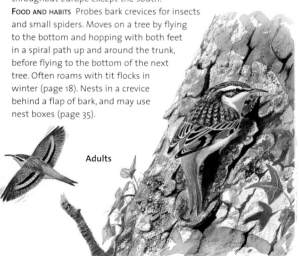

Adults

Nest usually behind
flap of thick bark

Adult (below)
feeding
juvenile

Juvenile

Method of
moving on and
between trees

Jay
Garrulus glandarius

SIZE AND DESCRIPTION Length 34cm. Striking bird with a pale eye, black moustaches and blue-and-black wing-flash. Streaked feathers on the forehead often raised in a crest. White rump obvious in flight.

VOICE Call a noisy screeching 'kscharch'.

HABITAT AND DISTRIBUTION Forests and parks throughout Europe. Often best seen in autumn when storing food.

Adults

FOOD AND HABITS Eats seeds, fruits, birds' eggs, nestlings and insects. Often congregates in small groups in autumn to collect and store nuts for winter. Buries acorns and beechnuts. May visit large gardens with tall trees. Nest is a shallow twiggy cup in the fork of a tree.

Head showing erect crest

Adult

Burying acorns

Magpie
Pica pica

SIZE AND DESCRIPTION Length 44cm, of which 20–30cm is tail. Wings metallic blue-black, and the long and round-tipped tail has a metallic-green sheen. Male larger than female, and tends to have a longer tail. Flight often a series of jerky flaps interspersed with swooping glides.
VOICE Noisy alarm call is a staccato rattle; also utters a variety of bisyllabic calls.
HABITAT AND DISTRIBUTION Breeds around farms and villages, and in hedgerows. Increasingly common in urban areas. Occurs across Europe except Iceland, northernmost Scotland and the far north of Norway.
FOOD AND HABITS Omnivorous; feeds on seeds, insects, carrion (often seen feeding on roadside casualties), nestlings and eggs. In winter, dozens of birds may congregate, noisily leaping through trees. Nest a dome of twigs high in a tree.

Roosts in flocks

Nesting

Adult

Fledglings

Adult

Juvenile

Jackdaw
Corvus monedula

SIZE AND DESCRIPTION Length 33cm. Nape grey and eye has a very pale iris. Juvenile is duller in colour than adult. Struts as it walks. In flight, wingbeats are faster and deeper than Carrion Crow's (page 160). Flies in flocks almost as densely as pigeons; flight often acrobatic.

VOICE Calls a metallic high-pitched 'kya' and 'chak'.

HABITAT AND DISTRIBUTION Found in fields, woods, farmland and towns across Europe.

FOOD AND HABITS Feeds on invertebrates, eggs, nestlings and grains. Breeds in tree hollows or on the ledges of buildings and cliffs, in pairs or small colonies.

Adults

Flight often acrobatic

Often roosts on rooftops

Tree-hole nest site

Juvenile

Rook
Corvus frugilegus

SIZE AND DESCRIPTION Length 46cm. Large black bird with 'ragged trousered' appearance. Bare face patch makes the bill seem very long. Purple gloss to plumage. Juvenile has an all-dark face and dark brown plumage.

VOICE Calls coarse and nasal, 'gaah' and 'grah'.

HABITAT AND DISTRIBUTION Farmland, both pasture and arable, with trees for nesting. Year-round resident in most of Europe, but summer visitor in the north and winter visitor in the south.

FOOD AND HABITS Eats mostly vegetable matter, seeds, roots, cereals and fruits; also a variety of animal foods. Not a common garden visitor and will only be seen in large rural gardens near rookeries. Breeds in colonies, erecting bulky twig nests in trees.

Searching for food on ground

Juvenile

Rookery

Adults

Adults

Carrion & Hooded Crows
Corvus corone & C. cornix

Characteristic pose while calling

May drop hard-cased foods, such as bones, from a height to smash the exteriors

Food includes carrion

SIZE AND DESCRIPTION Length 47cm. Totally black with a stout bill. Upper leg feathers neatly close-fitting. Juvenile much like adult, but duller. Hooded Crow (*C. cornix*), formerly regarded as the same species as Carrion Crow, is now recognized as a separate species.

VOICE Call a croaking 'krra-kra-kraa', more raucous than Rook's (page 158), and lower in pitch. Hooded Crow's voice is like Carrion Crow's.

HABITAT AND DISTRIBUTION Wide variety of habitats, from coasts to mountains and towns, throughout western and central Europe. Hooded Crow replaces Carrion Crow in eastern and northern Europe.

Adult Carrion
Crow

Adult Hooded
Crow

In Britain, it is common in north-west Scotland and Ireland, and rare on the east coast of England.

FOOD AND HABITS Omnivorous; feeds on carrion, nestlings and eggs, grain and insects. As its name suggests, eats a considerable amount of carrion such as roadkills. Not colonial. Nest is a bulky twig structure high up in the tree canopy. Food and habits of Hooded Crow as those of Carrion Crow.

Starling
Sturnus vulgaris

SIZE AND DESCRIPTION Length 21cm. Short tail and neck, upright stance, pink legs, white spots and a metallic green sheen. Non-breeding plumage has clear pale spots, which are reduced in breeding male. Breeding male also has a yellow bill; bill otherwise blackish. Juvenile grey-brown. Arrowhead profile in flight. Flocks fly in tight formation.
VOICE Versatile mimic of other birds. Calls are creaky twitters, chirps, clicks and whistles.
HABITAT AND DISTRIBUTION Widespread throughout Europe in all habitats, particularly human settlements. Has decreased alarmingly in Britain in the last few years and is now considered endangered.
FOOD AND HABITS Eats mainly leatherjackets and earthworms, and berries, seeds and fruits. Visits town gardens. Breeds in holes. Outside the breeding season roosts in huge flocks (page 19) in city buildings and trees.

Juvenile
moulting to
first-winter
plumage

Juvenile

Large autumn
pre-roost flight

Summer
adult

Probes ground
for earthworms
with long bill

House Sparrow
Passer domesticus

SIZE AND DESCRIPTION Length 15cm. Male has a grey cap and breast, and an extensive black throat-patch. Female has a pale brown cap and buff eyestripe. Wings of both sexes have small white wingbars.

VOICE Monotonous chirps; song a sequence of 'tshilp' and 'tshurrp' calls.

HABITAT AND DISTRIBUTION Completely linked to humans. Found in towns, villages and farmland near human habitation. Common but declining.

FOOD AND HABITS Omnivorous; feeds on seeds and insects, and bread and other food left by humans. In winter flocks feed in fields. Nests mostly on buildings, often colonially.

Male summer

Female

Male
display

Male autumn

Juvenile

Dust-bathing

Tree Sparrow
Passer montanus

SIZE AND DESCRIPTION Length 13cm. Sexes look similar. Distinguished from male House Sparrow (page 164) by its chestnut crown and nape, white cheeks, small, neat black bib and black spot behind the eye. Juvenile more subdued in colour than adult.

VOICE Song more musical than House Sparrow's.

HABITAT AND DISTRIBUTION Farmland and suburbs, but not a town bird. In winter flocks to feed in stubble fields with finches and buntings. Common in some parts of Europe. Increasingly scarce in Britain.

FOOD AND HABITS Feeds mainly on weed seeds and corn; also insects and spiders. Rare in cities, and mostly known from rural gardens. Visits bird tables for seeds and kitchen scraps. Autumn hedgerow-fruit crops are a favourite food. Nests in holes in trees, as well as in buildings. Uses nest boxes, but is highly susceptible to disturbance. Prefers to nest in colonies, so putting several boxes together may improve the chance of nesting.

Juvenile at nesthole

Adult

Nesting in nest box

Visiting Blackberry bush in autumn

Adults

Chaffinch
Fringilla coelebs

SIZE AND DESCRIPTION Length 15cm. In winter the blue-grey of the head and pink of the breast in male are subdued. Female similar to female House Sparrow (page 164). Two white bars on each wing.

VOICE Call a sharp 'pink'; flight call a softer 'yupp'. Song a loud, ringing trill that becomes lower, ends in a flourish and is then repeated.

HABITAT AND DISTRIBUTION Breeds in all types of woodland, and in parks and gardens. Flocks form in autumn. British Chaffinches are resident, but birds from elsewhere in Europe may winter in Britain.

FOOD AND HABITS Eats fruits and seeds, and also insects during the breeding season. Tends to feed on the ground in gardens, and may hop around beneath bird tables and feeders. Nest is a neat cup of moss, grass and feathers bound with spiders' webs, usually built in a tree fork.

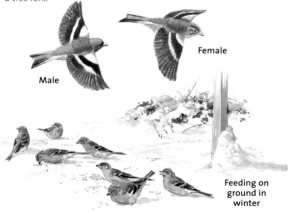

Male

Female

Feeding on
ground in
winter

Male
summer

Female

Male
winter

Brambling
Fringilla montifringilla

SIZE AND DESCRIPTION Length 15cm. In all plumages has an orange breast and a large white patch on the rump and lower back. Breeding male has a black head and bill. Female always has a brown-grey head.

VOICE Call a rasping 'zwee-ik'. Song simple and monotonous, like a distant saw, 'rrrrrhoo'.

HABITAT AND DISTRIBUTION Breeds in northern European forests. Occurs widely as a winter visitor in beech forests south to the Mediterranean.

FOOD AND HABITS Feeds on beechmast, seeds and berries, and insects in summer. Regularly visits feeders in gardens in favoured spots. Nest is a deep cup of moss, grass and hair, lined with feathers and wool, and decorated with bark and lichen; usually built in a tree fork.

Male winter

Female winter

Winter flock

Male winter

Male summer

Juvenile

Greenfinch
Carduelis chloris

SIZE AND DESCRIPTION Length 15cm. Summer male olive-green, merging into grey-green on the face, wings and flanks; bright yellow wing feathers on the sides of the tail. Female and juvenile paler with streaking, which is stronger in the latter. Bouncing, undulating flight.

VOICE Flight call a sharp 'burrurrup'. Song a wheezy sequence of twitters and whistles.

HABITAT AND DISTRIBUTION Breeds in woodland edges, open woodland, parks and gardens, and on farmland with hedges. Occurs year round in much of Europe.

FOOD AND HABITS Eats seeds and berries, and some insects during the breeding season. Visits feeders in gardens, favouring peanuts and sunflower seeds. Nest is a cup of grass, twigs and moss in a tree or bush.

Male

Female

Female

Male

Visiting
birdfeeder

Juvenile

Goldfinch
Carduelis carduelis

SIZE AND DESCRIPTION Length 13cm. Red face, white cheeks and throat, black cap and black-and-gold wings. In flight the wings show broad golden bands, and the white rump and black tail are visible. Sexes alike, but juvenile has a brown-streaked head.

VOICE Cheerful trisyllabic 'tickelitt' call. Song a series of rapid trills and twitters.

HABITAT AND DISTRIBUTION Open lowland woodland, heaths, orchards and gardens in most of Europe.

FOOD AND HABITS Eats seeds and berries. Favours teasels and thistle heads, from which it extracts seeds with its specially adapted bill. Also eats insects during the breeding season. Visits garden feeders, favouring niger and sunflower seeds. Nest is made of hair and rootlets, and positioned high in the tree canopy.

Adults

Juvenile

Extraordinarily agile when extracting seeds from thistle heads

Visits feeders to take niger seeds

Bullfinch
Pyrrhula pyrrhula

SIZE AND DESCRIPTION Length 16cm. Compact, bull-necked finch with
a black cap. Male has a rosy red breast, grey back, white rump and
black tail. Female has a pale brown breast. Juvenile has a grey-brown
head and breast. Northern race *P. p. pyrrhula* differs from British race
P. p. pileata in being larger, the males greyer above and lighter red
below, the females greyer on the upperparts and paler below. White

Male
pyrrhula
race

Juvenile

Female
pyrrhula
race

wingbars of both sexes show in flight, which is fast and undulating.
Voice Call a soft and sad fluted whistle. Northern race *P. p. pyrrhula* has a trumpeting call.

Habitat and distribution Mixed woodland, parks, large gardens and churchyards. Feeds in orchards and gardens. Widespread and resident throughout Europe, except in the far south.

Food and habits Feeds on buds and seeds, and insects in the breeding season. May visit feeders in undisturbed gardens with Blackthorn and fruit trees. Nest is a shallow platform of twigs built in a shrub.

Female Male

Male
pileata race

Flower buds
are favourite
foods

Female
pileata race

Hawfinch
Coccothraustes coccothraustes

Adults

Male

Female

Juvenile

SIZE AND DESCRIPTION Length 18cm. Big head, huge bill and short tail. Male has a russet-toned head with black feathering around the bill base and chin. Grey nape and collar merge into a rich mahogany mantle, fading into a russet rump and central tail. Outer tail and tail tips are white, and wings have a broad white wingbar and bluish flight feathers. Female generally duller and more grey-brown than male. Bill in both sexes blue-black in summer, becoming brown in winter. Juvenile a greyish-brown, scaly version of adults. Wingbars are visible in flight.

VOICE Call a sharp 'tic'. Song a soft series of 'zih' and 'zri' notes.

HABITAT AND DISTRIBUTION Deciduous and mixed woodland. More widespread and confiding on the Continent than in Britain.

FOOD AND HABITS Feeds on seeds, cherry stones and nuts. Rare visitor to British gardens, and most likely to be observed early in the morning, particularly in the vicinity of Hornbeams, the species' favourite tree. Nest is a bulky twig platform high in the tree canopy.

Serin
Serinus serinus

Males

Size and description Length 11cm. Smallest finch, with a tiny conical bill. Male yellow-green with dark streaks, a bright yellow head and breast, and a yellow rump; breast becomes brighter as it wears. Female rather duller.

Voice Song has a jingling quality.

Habitat and distribution Gardens, parks and churchyards. Rare in Britain, breeding very occasionally, mostly in Devon, Dorset and East Anglia; common in central and southern Europe.

Food and habits Mostly eats plant seeds, including those of alder and birch. Rare in gardens in Britain. Nest is a tiny cup of grass and moss high up in a tree.

Siskin
Carduelis spinus

SIZE AND DESCRIPTION Length 12cm. Dark-streaked greenish-yellow plumage. Male yellower than female, with a black cap and bib. Wingbars in both sexes are yellow, and male's tail has yellow patches on either side. Tail deeply notched. Flight flitting and uneven.

VOICE Flight call either a descending 'tilu' or a rising 'tlui'. Twittery and trilling song.

HABITAT AND DISTRIBUTION Coniferous and mixed forests in winter in much of Europe.

FOOD AND HABITS Feeds on seeds of trees. Once rare in gardens, Siskins have become regular winter visitors in many areas. They are very acrobatic and compete with each other at birdfeeders. Nest is a cup of twigs high up in a tree, usually a conifer.

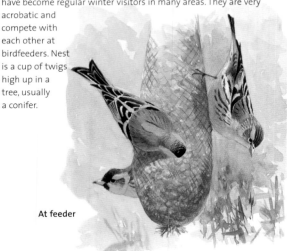

At feeder

Males

Female

Juvenile

Lesser & Mealy Redpolls
Carduelis caberet & C. flammea

SIZE AND DESCRIPTION Length 12cm. Greyish-brown and dark-streaked with a red forehead and small black bib; small broad bill. Adult male has a red upper breast. Wings have faint wingbars. Juvenile lacks the red head. Mealy Redpoll (*C. flammea*), found in Scandinavia, is slightly larger, and paler and less brown.

Female

Male
summer

VOICE Flight call a hard metallic 'chet-chet-chet'.

HABITAT AND DISTRIBUTION Breeds in forests (especially birch) and on heaths from Britain to southern Scandinavia and western central Europe. Mealy Redpoll is a rare winter visitor to northern and eastern Britain.

FOOD AND HABITS Feeds in flocks, searching among the tips of birch trees for seeds. Eats insects in the breeding season. Visits gardens with birch or alder in winter, and mixes with Siskins and Goldfinches. Nest is a neat cup high in a tree.

Mealy Redpoll
female

Mealy Redpoll
male

Male
winter

Linnet
Carduelis cannabina

SIZE AND DESCRIPTION Length 13cm. Breeding male has a crimson forehead and breast, and a chestnut mantle. Winter male resembles female.

VOICE Canary-like song is a pleasant twitter consisting of chirping and rolling sounds, sung from the top of a bush.

HABITAT AND DISTRIBUTION Open fields with bushes and waste ground. Farmland and coasts in winter. Widespread throughout most of Europe. Common but declining due to changes in agricultural practices.

FOOD AND HABITS Mostly eats seeds and arable weeds. A small amount of insects is taken during breeding. Favours bushy rural gardens and town gardens adjoining wasteground. Often breeds in loose colonies. Nest is a grassy cup well hidden in a shrub.

Feeds in flocks

Female

Juvenile

Male
summer

Male
winter

Yellowhammer
Emberiza citrinella

SIZE AND DESCRIPTION Length 16cm. Male has a vivid yellow head, brown-streaked back and chestnut rump. Female is duller. Extent of yellow in the plumage varies depending on the time of year and sex of the bird.
VOICE Song a jingling phrase on one note, 'a little bit of bread and no cheese'.

Males

Female

HABITAT AND DISTRIBUTION Arable farmland grassland with banks or hedges. In winter flocks to feed in stubble fields and farmyards. Widespread in much of continental Europe as well as Britain, but declining due to modern intensive farming methods, which have removed many essential foods.

FOOD AND HABITS Feeds on grasses, seeds and fruits; also insects. Visits large rural gardens near mature hedgerows and forest edges. In winter often feeds with mixed flocks of finches and buntings, and may visit gardens to feed on spilt seeds on the ground. Nest is a cup of grass low in a shrub.

Juvenile

Female/ juvenile

Males

Female/ juvenile

Reed Bunting
Emberiza schoeniclus

SIZE AND DESCRIPTION Length 15cm. Summer male has a rich brown back streaked darker, grey-brown rump, blackish tail with white outer feathers and whitish upperparts. Crown and face are black, with a white collar running into white moustachial streaks; throat and upper breast are also black. Winter male, female and juvenile are less boldly marked.

VOICE Call 'tsee-you'. Song a repetitive 'tsit tsit tsrit tsrelitt'.

HABITAT AND DISTRIBUTION Marshes, scrub and farmland in much of Europe.

FOOD AND HABITS Feeds mainly on seeds. Like Yellowhammer (page 186) may visit large rural gardens in the vicinity of its natural habitat to feed on seeds. Often perches on reed stems and telegraph wires. Nest is a grassy cup concealed low in vegetation.

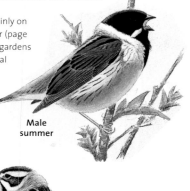

Male summer

Female winter

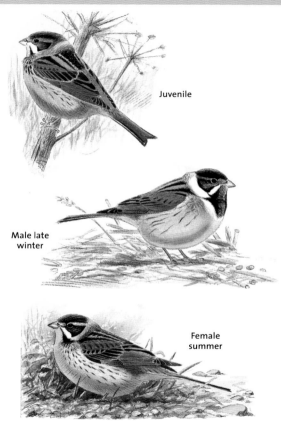

Juvenile

Male late winter

Female summer

Index

Bird Topography

Some of the key terms used to describe the different parts of birds.

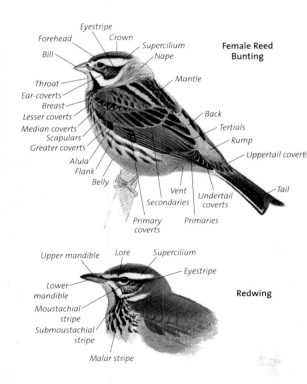

Female Reed Bunting

Eyestripe
Forehead
Crown
Supercilium
Nape
Bill
Mantle
Throat
Ear-coverts
Breast
Back
Lesser coverts
Tertials
Median coverts
Rump
Scapulars
Greater coverts
Uppertail covert
Alula
Flank
Belly
Tail
Vent
Secondaries
Undertail coverts
Primaries
Primary coverts

Redwing

Upper mandible
Lore
Supercilium
Eyestripe
Lower mandible
Moustachial stripe
Submoustachial stripe
Malar stripe